ONE MORNING IN THE WAR

RICHARD HAMMER

053714

One Morning in the War

THE TRAGEDY AT SON MY

Coward-McCann, Inc., New York

Copyright © 1970 by Richard Hammer

All rights reserved. This book, or parts thereof, may not be reproduced in any form without permission in writing from the publisher. Published on the same day in Canada by Longmans Canada Limited, Toronto.

Library of Congress Catalog
Card Number: 78–121323
PRINTED IN THE UNITED STATES OF AMERICA
BY AMERICAN BOOK–STRATFORD PRESS, INC.

For
Peter Matson

Contents

To plunder, to slaughter, to steal, these things they misname empire; and where they make a desert, they call it peace.

—TACITUS, *Agricola*

The triumph of the man who kills or tortures is marred by only one shadow: he is unable to feel that he is innocent. Thus he must create guilt in his victim so that, in a world that has no direction, universal guilt will authorize no other course of action than the use of force and give its blessing to nothing but success. When the concept of innocence disappears from the mind of the innocent victim himself, the value of power establishes a definitive rule over a world in despair. That is why an unworthy and cruel penitence reigns over this world where only the stones are innocent.

—ALBERT CAMUS, *The Rebel*

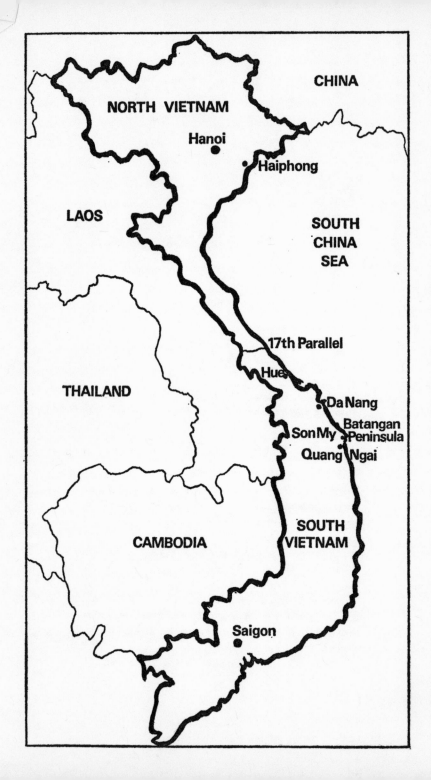

Introduction

FOR many Americans, and for many people around the world who love or hate America, the revelation that American soldiers massacred several hundred Vietnamese civilians at the village of Son My on March 16, 1968, has been traumatic. It has forced some to re-evaluate their views about the United States, to question seriously for the first time many of the things this country has done in Vietnam. It has caused others to bury their heads deeper and to close their minds even tighter, to deny the events or to find specious reasons to excuse them. And there were those who welcomed the opportunity to condemn a whole nation.

In reality it did not take Son My to crystalize such reactions. Son My was just another one of many such catalysts arising from the war in Vietnam. While the events at Son My cannot be dismissed, or ignored, conversely, they must not be blown out of proportion either. They must be looked at in perspective within the proper frame of reference.

It has not been my purpose in this book to excuse, to blame or to condemn individuals. Instead I have tried to discover, not reasons to love, hate or excuse the United States, but rather how and why an atrocity, the massacre at Son My village, could occur, and how and why American soldiers sent to protect and defend a people could turn and slaughter them.

In attempting to do this I realized that it was not enough to describe the events of that March 16th in isolation. They did not occur in some vacuum unrelated to or uninfluenced by events before them. And so in these pages, to try to understand that morning, I have tried to look at the American soldier in Vietnam with his fears, hatred, and desires; to look at the Vietnamese in the hamlet with his desires, fears and hatreds; and to try to see how that day fit—or did not fit—into the whole nature of the struggle in Vietnam and the American involvement there.

During the research for this book both in Vietnam and in the United States, a number of things came to my attention which had not yet been made public—and some of them at this time still seem to be buried. I discovered, for instance, after talking with both Vietnamese and Americans, and after examining reports of the action that day and studying Vietnamese and American military maps of the area that the American troops involved in the action at Son My village had actually attacked the wrong hamlet, not the one where the Viet Cong were centered. This information was given by me to the American military authorities in both Vietnam and the United States. In somewhat different form from this book, I described in a *Look* magazine article how and why this occurred.

It also became apparent to me that there had been not one but two separate and distinct massacres that morning in the hamlets of Son My village. I informed a high official of the army's investigating committee of this early in January of 1970; he did not seem overly appreciative of this information. Nevertheless, about a month later, the officer in charge of that other platoon was charged with murder. Though the army has not revealed the details of that action, the reader will find them in the pages of this book.

There is, in addition, considerable other information about both the Americans and the Vietnamese, particularly in Son My, about which most Americans still seem unaware.

Throughout this book, I have used Vietnamese spelling of

place names. It seemed the natural and correct thing to do, when describing events that happened in Vietnam, and because, as I have tried to show in these pages, terrible misfortune can arise from ignoring the names that the indigenous people gave their homes. Thus, while many American newspapers persist in spelling Vietnamese place names as one word—i.e., Sonmy, Mylai, etc.—I have followed the Vietnamese practice of spelling them as two words.

And a special note on Son My. For some reason which I have been unable to discover—perhaps it was the slip of a finger on a telegraph key or a teletype machine in Saigon when the story first broke—the American press has persisted in calling the village that was the scene of the massacre either Song My or Songmy. On all Vietnamese maps, in all Vietnamese writings, it is Son My, without the "g." The word "song" in Vietnamese means "river." There are, of course, many "songs" in Vietnam, but there are, as far as I was able to discover, no villages named "river." Thus to call this village Song My is to call it the My River, and that it is not. Rather it is Son, a word meaning "mountain" or "hill." Just as in the United States, there are many villages named after mountains. Thus, again, I have chosen to use the Vietnamese name for the village—Son My.

Acknowledgments

THERE are a great many people to whom I owe debts which can never be paid. Without their help during the research and writing of this book, I would have been totally lost. So it is only just that some of them, at least, be mentioned here. Yet they bear no responsibility for the use of the information here nor for any of the failings of this book. Those are mine alone.

Perhaps the first and possibly as important as anyone else, is Duong The Tu, who served as my interpreter while I was in Vietnam; who travelled with me to Quang Ngai, to the scene of the massacre and to the refugee camps; who came often to anticipate my questions and extend them; whose ability to find people and to win their confidence was invaluable; and who, above all, became a good friend. Then there was Lieutenant Colonel Russ Whitla, chief of the U.S. Joint Public Affairs Office in Quang Ngai city, who was unfailingly helpful, who gave us the use of his jeep, who called for transportation when we requested it, who never in any way interfered with us in our travels in and out of the city, and on whose living room couches we slept for many nights. Major Pauli and Captain Johnson and their aides at the Americal Division headquarters in Chu Lai made transportation arrangements for us to Quang Ngai, and spent many hours briefing us on the army's view of the situation in the I Corps area and in Quang Ngai. Various officers at JUSPAO and at the Military Assistance Command-Vietnam headquarters in Saigon were continuously helpful and did their best to ease my way through much red tape. Terry Smith and the other members of *The New York Times* bureau in Saigon gave me so much good advice and help that I would have been lost without them.

Then there are many people whose names I cannot mention, including a number of Vietnamese who might get into serious trouble if they had been quoted by name, and so I have not done so, though their information and their discussions with me were invaluable. Several men at American Division headquarters in Chu Lai showed me photographs, tipped me to leads and gave me much information without permission and might well find themselves in considerable trouble with the army if I were to single them out by name. Members of Charley Company talked to me openly on condition that I not mention their names or credit any statements directly to them; I have done what they asked and I will continue to abide by their wishes.

A number of other people helped in the United States: Daniel Schwarz, the Sunday Editor, and Jack Desmond, the Assistant Sunday Editor, of *The New York Times* gave me leave of absence to go to Vietnam and again, later, to write this book; Ellis Amburn, my editor, has been unflappably enthusiastic, full of suggestions and patient; and many, many others, too numerous to mention. And finally, there are my wife, Nina, and my sons who lived with me through this when I was short-tempered, absent-minded, oblivious to them and their needs, and did not complain.

—R.H.
Saigon—Quang Ngai—New York

PART ONE

The Village of Son My

ONCE there was a village in Vietnam. It was called Son My. It lay along the shores of the South China Sea in Quang Ngai Province in what had once been the Kingdom of Annam and is now the northern part of the Republic of Vietnam (South Vietnam). The land was marshy and fertile, yielding two rich harvests of rice each year. The sea was inexhaustibly stocked with fish and the people used to say that their nets would fill even before they were cast into the water. The beaches were broad and beautiful, with soft velvet textured sand; some villagers, with local pride, called them the most beautiful in all Vietnam, and vacationers came regularly from Quang Ngai city and some even from as far away as Saigon, nearly three hundred and fifty miles to the south, to bask on the sands and swim in the warm sea.

Once nearly ten thousand people lived in the village of Son My, in its four hamlets and twenty sub-hamlets scattered amid the rice paddies and rivers covering more than twenty square miles from the Song Cho Mai (Cho Mai River) on the north, just below the Batangan Peninsula, to the wide and meandering Song Tra Khuc (Tra Khuc River) on the south; from the sea on the east inland three or four miles to the west. Except for two small hills in the southern part of the village—Nui Da Voi, or Elephant Hill, from the shape some people said they saw in its humped and convoluted ridges, and Nui Ngura, or Horse Mountain, for some people in the village used to say that it looked like the head of a stallion—the flat land gave rise only to palm trees and bamboo, to scrubby growth and the high hedge-rows that surrounded and protected the numberless rice paddies.

Once life was good and satisfying for the people of Son My. They were independent, proud and self-sufficient, with plenty of rice and fish to eat and enough left to take to market to sell and then return home with cloth and sandals and the few other necessities of their lives. They had a saying in the village in those days: "In January we enjoy our children. In February we enjoy our beaches. In March we enjoy our fairs." For the rest of the year there was hard work in the paddies and on the fishing grounds, but the earth and the sea provided.

On March 16, 1968, in the hours before noon, the village of Son My died. That morning, American troops in what was called Task Force Barker came to Son My. With them came bombs and artillery shells, small arms fire and grenades, torches and rockets. When Task Force Barker left Son My, the houses were leveled, the fields and ripening crops laid waste, the live-stock slaughtered, the people scattered throughout Quang Ngai Province and throughout all of South Vietnam, squatters in refugee camps.

The dead were left behind. When Task Force Barker aban-doned Son My, more than five hundred people—men, women and children—had been deliberately and indiscriminately slaugh-tered in three small sub-hamlets of the village. They had been massacred in two separate actions by two different companies of the task force.

The first to feel the blow were two small sub-hamlets of the hamlet of Tu Cung in the western part of Son My. These sub-hamlets were called Xom Lang—a name which means only the hamlet, and so the people called it more poetically, because tranquility seemed to be its innate nature, Thuan Yen, or Peace, The Place Where Trouble Does Not Come—and Binh Dong,

4

separated by less than five hundred meters. At about seven that morning, Company C of the First Battalion, Twentieth Infantry, Eleventh Infantry Brigade, Twenty-Third Infantry Division (called the Americal Division) fell on Xom Lang and Binh Dong. In less than an hour, the two sub-hamlets were destroyed and, according to those who survived, about four hundred and thirty-five people were killed.

About two hours later, to the east in a sub-hamlet of the hamlet of Co Luy, called My Hoi, a platoon of Company B of the task force engaged in a distinct and separate rampage. According to survivors of My Hoi, some of whom had returned to it only the night before after years of exile in refugee camps, between ninety-seven and a hundred people fell there to the small arms fire and grenades of the Americans.

For the Americans, at first, it was a famous victory. At least that's what it seemed that Sunday afternoon of March 17, 1968, when the first reports came out of the Americal Division's headquarters in Chu Lai, to the north of Quang Ngai, which were then amplified by spokesmen for the United States Military Assistance Command-Vietnam at the afternoon press briefing in Saigon.

This was right after the sudden Viet Cong onslaughts of the Tet Offensive in February. By mid-March, the Viet Cong had pulled back with heavy losses and the Americans were once again on the attack, mounting intensive search-and-destroy missions to seek out and kill Viet Cong and North Vietnamese Army troops throughout the south. The technique was to attack centers of VC strength, to move the civilian population to safer, protected camps where they could be both guarded and watched by American and Army of the Republic of Vietnam (ARVN) troops, to destroy the houses, crops and animals in the villages and so deny the Viet Cong and the North Vietnamese Army food, shelter and protection.

The area east of the provincial capital of Quang Ngai was just such a VC stronghold. According to reports received by the American military intelligence, elements of the 48th Viet Cong Local Force Battalion (a VC battalion is about five hundred men), considered one of the toughest units in the entire VC army, were operating from the village of Son My. Its center in the village was what was marked on American military maps as My Lai (1), a sub-hamlet on the coast of the South China Sea. On these maps, the settlement was colored in pink, and so the army familiarly called it—as it called all such settlements colored pink on the maps, and there were many of them—"Pinkville," though nowhere was the name Pinkville written.

For Vietnamese, however, the name of this sub-hamlet was My Khe in the hamlet of My Lai, itself a section of the village of Son My. The Vietnamese had no knowledge that the Americans had renamed it, though they knew that most Vietnamese names, particularly those of small sub-hamlets, were unknown and meaningless to the Americans.

The object of the operation that day, of Task Force Barker—itself a unit in the larger and more far-ranging Operation Muscatine—was to attack the VC concentration, wipe it out and destroy it and all of Son My and move any civilians who happened to be there.

Taking the reports that came in from Company C on the night of March 16, the press officer of the brigade, working in Chu Lai, wrote a press release on the operation for dissemination the next day. He reported: "Jungle warriors together with artillery and helicopter support hit the village of My Lai early yesterday morning. Contacts throughout the morning and early afternoon resulted in 128 enemy killed, 13 suspects detained and three weapons captured."

Later, nearly two years later, the press officer, Arthur Dunn, was to say that he felt there was something "fishy" about the information on which he based his release. The reports from the task force "raised questions in my mind" as to just how the Viet Cong could have carried away all its other weapons from such a major engagement at close-quarters.

In Saigon, at the "five o'clock follies," as the afternoon press briefing is called, the American Army spokesmen that Sunday gave out a few more details to questioning reporters. During the action, the spokesman said, two Americans had been killed somewhere in the area and ten had been wounded. This was the first—and only—report of American casualties in the operation.

As *The New York Times* reported it in a front page story Monday morning the American version of the assault on Son My, as relayed from the military in Saigon went like this:

". . . The fighting erupted six miles northeast of Quangngai in the area of sand dunes and scrub brush between Highway 1 and the South China Sea. . . .

". . . about 150 men of the Americal Division encountered the enemy force early yesterday. A second company from the same unit was dropped in by helicopter two miles to the northeast to provide a squeeze on the enemy troops.

"The United States soldiers were sweeping the area, where numerous clashes had been fought in the last year and a half, but which had been relatively quiet in recent months, with the exception of the Lunar New Year attack on the city of Quangngai [sic] itself.

"The operation is another American offensive to clear enemy pockets still threatening the cities.

"The area was heavily shelled by artillery at dawn yesterday before the troops moved in on foot.

"While the two companies of United States soldiers moved in on the enemy force from opposite sides, heavy artillery barrages and armed helicopters were called in to pound the North Vietnamese soldiers.

7

"The American command's military communiqué said fighting continued sporadically through the day. The action ended at 3 P.M. when the remaining North Vietnamese slipped out and fled, according to the communiqué.

"It was not made clear how many of the enemy had been killed by the artillery and helicopter attacks and how many were shot down by the American infantrymen."

Though no one questioned it at the time, the statement by the military that they met North Vietnamese soldiers, should have led to further and pointed inquiries. This area along the coast had long been deemed Viet Cong territory. Few if any regular NVA troops had as yet been seen that far east in Quang Ngai Province. Save for a few Viet Cong scouts and guides assigned to steer the North Vietnamese in the right direction through country with which they were just as unfamiliar as were the Americans, the Viet Cong and the North Vietnamese Army operated on most occasions separately. In what was strong Viet Cong country, the North Vietnamese were not often seen. There was a certain amount of jealousy and friction between NVA and VC; neither wanted to take orders from the other and, at this time in 1968, neither had yet been so badly decimated that they needed re-inforcements from the other. Thus, while the VC operated throughout Vietnam, the major centers of its activities were within the territory along the coast where most of the population lived. The NVA tended to center its base of operations away from the major population centers, that is to the west and the mountains. This has changed since mid-1968, as casualties grew, and today mixed VC-NVA units are found everywhere. But in 1968 such was not the case. If the American Army had fought NVA troops that morning along the coast, as the news reports had it, it should have created more than a little furor in the American military circles, especially in the intelligence. It would have been an unexpected clash and perhaps a

8

disturbing one, for it would have revealed the NVA in an area where it was not known to be. But the report created no stir. For the enemy that morning was not NVA. This was still, along the sea, VC territory and enemy found there were VC.

The victory was celebrated again, on August 1, 1968, in the weekly newspaper of the Americal Division, "The Southern Cross." In a long article celebrating recent victories by the division, and illustrated with photographs of slim, trim American boys winning their war (some of them taken at Son My by Ronald Haeberle, an American soldier-photographer assigned on March 16 to Company C), the division reporter enthusiastically glowed:

"Operation Muscatine involved some of the largest encounters with the Viet Cong in the Warrior's fledgling history. Troops twice encountered a Viet Cong battalion near the village of My Lai and killed a total of 196 enemy soldiers.

"When Task Force Barker was disbanded after 78 days, it had accounted for 401 of the 1,000-plus enemy killed in the six months of fighting in the Muscatine area."

Celebrated and recorded for posterity and the division's annals, the victory at Son My faded and was forgotten.

Forgotten, that is, until September 6, 1969, nearly eighteen months after the assault. On that day, in newspaper offices and broadcasting studios around the United States, a small story, less than a hundred words long, clattered across the Associated Press ticker.

"FORT BENNING, GA. (AP)—AN ARMY OFFICER HAS BEEN CHARGED WITH MURDER IN THE DEATHS OF AN UNSPECIFIED NUMBER OF CIVILIANS IN VIET NAM [sic] IN 1968, POST AUTHORITIES HAVE REVEALED.

"COL. DOUGLAS TUCKER, INFORMATION OFFICER, SAID THE CHARGE WAS BROUGHT FRIDAY

AGAINST 1ST LT. WILLIAM L. CALLEY JR., 26, OF MIAMI, FLA., A TWO-YEAR VETERAN WHO WAS TO HAVE BEEN DISCHARGED FROM THE SERVICE SATURDAY."

What had not been discovered then, and would not be discovered for many more months, was that the scene of these murders, the scene of what would soon be called a massacre, was not the place American troops should have attacked.

The major goal of Task Force Barker that morning was what the Americans called among themselves—though nowhere in any order or on any map was it so called—"Pinkville." This was the sub-hamlet of My Khe in the hamlet of My Lai, a fishing settlement on the coast. According to all information, and according to later statements by the people who lived in Son My village, the VC were centered at My Khe, and de facto controlled the settlement. This was what was labeled on the American maps as My Lai (1) and shaded in pink.

But instead of landing in the fields and paddies outside this VC stronghold, bombarding it, attacking it and catching the VC in the pincers of American troops on three sides and the sea on the fourth, the helicopters that morning set down outside what was marked on the military maps as My Lai (4), about three kilometers (less than two miles) inland and to the west of My Khe or Pinkville.

The soldiers of the first platoon of Charley Company went in shooting, and for nearly an hour they did not stop. They were convinced they were attacking Pinkville, or My Lai, the VC stronghold (and some of them still think so). They were prepared for heavy action and large casualties. Instead, they hit the sub-hamlet of Xom Lang, or Thuan Yen, in the hamlet of Tu Cung, a hamlet which if not considered exactly friendly was, nevertheless, not considered implacably hostile. On the American military maps, it was called My Lai (4).

By the margin of error of less than two miles, and perhaps because of the mis-naming by the Americans, a settlement which was not the center of the VC, where the VC had never appeared in great numbers, was the first to suffer that morning, and suffer in the extreme. Dire trouble had come to The Place Where Trouble Does Not Come.

To see Xom Lang, to see all of Son My as it was once, to begin to understand what it meant to those who lived there, and to attempt to comprehend what happened that morning in March, one must see Xom Lang, see Son My, as it is today, see its desolation and talk with those who have fled it.

But that is no easy thing to do. There is about Quang Ngai Province, as there is about much of Vietnam outside Saigon, the ambience of the frontier, with all its perils and uncertainties, and travel from one place to another is not without its dangers.

It is less than eight miles by road from the city of Quang Ngai, the provincial capital of fifty thousand people (at least a quarter of them refugees living in squalid camps deposited in the muddy swamps of every vacant field in and around the city), east to the beach, to the place where the village of Son My once stood. But to make that journey in these days of war is to trek into the wilderness from the relative safety of an armed bastion, to venture into the kind of territory American troops in Vietnam call "Indian Country."

Quang Ngai city is the headquarters of the Second Division of the ARVN, and it sometimes seems that every other adult male is in a modified and rakish olive green American-style uniform (made distinctive by a trimmer cut and, often, a red scarf knotted around the neck), splattered with mud and dirt from the unpaved streets of the city. The buildings, in a kind of bastard French colonial rococo, are patinated with dust and fading, peeling paint. And, strangely, the city seems to have over it the aura of a wild west cavalry post in the 1870's, moved to Asia and only slightly modernized.

Trucks filled with soldiers and the equipment of war rumble through Quang Ngai, down the main street, a black concrete and paved belt cutting through the center of the city on its way from Saigon in the south to Da Nang and Hue, about seventy miles north, in a steady, endless caravan. This is Highway Number One.

The commercial center of Quang Ngai, concentrated within a few blocks, is a jumble of two-story wooden buildings, the wood chipped, cracked and broken, the paint shredding. The ground floors are all open and on the broad dirt sidewalk in front of them there are stalls. All are filled with an indiscriminate mixture of Vietnamese goods—straw hats, clothing, food—imported necessities—B. F. Goodrich sandals, Air Vietnam flight bags, caps and hats of all kinds—and the luxuries straight from the United States Army Post Exchange—cigarettes, radios, watches, lighters, fatigues. The crowds are thick, moving slowly, picking through the merchandise and incessantly haggling over price.

Beyond the commercial center almost every corner is blocked by coils of barbed concertina wire and a sandbagged ARVN checkpoint. The sentries, some drowsy and some alert and nervous in their shelters, poise over machine guns.

The air echoes with the constant boom of artillery, though always muted and somewhere in the distance. These days almost all the shells are outgoing. There are sporadic, sudden and sharp clatters of small arms and machine gun fire, nearer but usually somewhere out of range, to the west and the mountains, to the east and the sea. In the sky there are often the vapor trails of jets, and if one follows the trails down toward the horizon, he will see the jets darting low, diving and then pulling up and soaring away. Long after they have vanished, the sound of the rockets or the bombs will echo in the air. Off on the horizon, too, one can often see helicopter gun ships poised, motionless, over some spot vacated by the jets.

Still, even on what one is told and soon comes to believe is a dangerous frontier, and despite the war and its ominous ever-presence, a city is a city, somehow removed and isolated, an island whose fringes are tossed by the storm but whose center remains calm, but on edge. The women, like those in Saigon and the other big cities, are slim and graceful with a delicate beauty, dressed in the flowing yet form-fitting au dais—the long white or colored slitted gowns and the black or white trousers. The men, those not in uniform, wear city clothes—dark trousers, white shirts and fedoras of straw or felt or canvas. They are concerned not with the war but with commerce. There are the bureaucrats, Vietnamese and Americans, pondering the papers that contain the destiny of the province under government rule; they sit in dim light, for the electricity often does not work, at desks in the seedy and crumbling provincial buildings.

And there are, of course, the thousands of refugees. But they do not seem to intrude on the life of the city. Like pariahs, bringing with them uncomfortable visions and disturbing thoughts which the city wants to forget or not think about, they are isolated. They remain in their camps, down mud trails, uncertain, wondering how to feed and shelter their children and when, if ever, they will be able to return home.

Out of the city, the world changes and the war comes closer. The road to the beach, to Xom Lang and Son My, branches off Highway Number One just across a long and carefully guarded bridge, with sandbagged emplacements at both ends and in the middle, over the murky and (except in the rainy season) shallow Song Tra Khuc. Within a few hundred yards, after passing through the market at An Phu, also surrounded by

13

refugee camps,* the cutoff becomes a narrow, twisting, rutted dirt lane—a quagmire in the rainy season. It is wide enough only for a jeep, and a jeep is about the only vehicle that could traverse it other than horse-drawn carts or the ubiquitous Yamahas, Hondas and other Japanese motorbikes and the bicycles from France, England, and Japan. The road twists, winding between small hills to the north, dotted on the highest slopes with Buddhist cemeteries and then, below, with terraced rice paddies falling like flights of steps to the road, and on the south with more rice paddies falling in terraces to the Tra Khuc River. The paddies, filled with mirror-still water, glisten in the daylight, the light refracting off the surface; from the distance, during the planting season when the rice has not yet grown over the water level, they seem like large chips of pastel tiles set in the earth, pale purples and blues and pinks and greens. Once they were separated from each other by high hedgerows. But when the Americans came, the hedgerows provided too much concealment for the VC to hide behind—"A whole VC company could be in one of those paddies hiding behind the hedgerows and you could walk right by on patrol and never even know they were there," an American major says—and so they were cut down; now the fields are separated only by mounds of earth or by low hedges, the height of a man's waist. The farmers in the paddies, stooped, dressed usually in the traditional black pajamas—tunic and trousers gathered at the ankles—their faces hidden beneath the wide cones of their straw hats (are they men or women or children? one cannot tell) do not turn or look up when a vehicle crawls by. Standing knee-deep, hip-deep in the water-filled paddies, they labor on steadily and slowly, rising, falling, moving with a ritual deliberation.

* In 1967, there were estimates that more than twenty-five per cent of the Vietnamese population then lived in refugee camps, driven from their homes by the war. The figure is now thought to be closer to fifty per cent.

Within a few miles, the road widens as it comes to another market surrounded by more refugee camps. This is Chau Thanh, the ruins of an ancient citadel built by mandarins about eight hundred years ago and destroyed after it had stood less than three hundred years. The road and the market swirl with milling people picking their way through the open stalls which march back from the outer rubbled walls of the old citadel toward the low hills beyond. The jeep's horn blows. The people, a few of them, turn and look, bend backward reluctantly; the jeep threads its way slowly through the crowd and then is into the open.

For a way past the old citadel there are more paddies, meticulously groomed so that one almost thinks he is looking at a painting superimposed on the land. But now there are fewer Vietnamese on motorbikes or bicycles, fewer pedestrians along the sides of the road. The walkers one does see are moving quickly. They are peasants, wearing the short black tunics and black trousers and wide conical hats, carrying long bamboo poles with baskets balanced at the ends across their shoulders; they are on their way to market or, having finished, hurrying home.

The road veers right, drops suddenly into a deep ditch filled, except in the dry season, with stagnant muddy water. A couple of Vietnamese are bathing their feet or washing the mud of the road from their bikes. They do not move. The jeep turns, veers, slides through the ditch around them and up the steep other side, back onto the track. It was here, when the VC arrived, one is told, that the road was cut and the VC gained almost total control of the territory to the east, all the way to the sea.

It takes the eye a moment to adjust, to accept the change. The carefully cultivated paddies are gone. Except for an occasional solitary quickly moving walker at the side of the road, there is no one. To the north and south of the road there is desolation, a wilderness overgrown, new trees beginning to push their way through the soft green turf, old palm trees, some fallen, some with the tops blasted away so that they stand naked and forelorn, making one somehow abashed and wanting to avert ones eyes. What must once have been paddies are now filled with weeds, laying fallow. In the distance one can make out depressions in the earth. Craters? Over there is what could be rubble, or maybe just bare spots.

This is "Indian Country," then. It is country where a fire fight could erupt on any night, or even during the day if something is sighted moving and that something turns out to be VC and not a water buffalo. It is country where the VC—and lately some units of the NVA—hide in bunkers and tunnels so intricate and hidden so well that one could walk over them and not realize they were there. It is country where these same VC and NVA emerge in the darkness to roam the ravaged countryside. It is country where a tin can or a piece of paper or anything lying loose could be a booby trap, where any piece of ground could conceal a land mine. It is the kind of place called a free fire zone; anything that moves here is the enemy and can be—and will be—shot at with all the massive firepower at the command of the Americans and the ARVN.

One has come to the borders of what used to be the village of Son My. From here to the sea, extending north and south to the rivers is where the village once stood and now stands nothing. This part of the village, at its western edge, was once the hamlet of Tu Cung, one of the four that made up the village. And just north of the road is Tu Cung's sub-hamlet of Xom Lang, upon which the Americans fell that March morning. A couple of hundred meters beyond is the sub-hamlet of Binh Dong, which, like Xom Lang, was to bear witness to American firepower and enmity.

At dawn on that March morning in 1968, about five hundred

people lived in these sub-hamlets. Most of them were old men, women and children, for the young men, in their late teens and early twenties, were away, some with the VC, some with the ARVN, some just gone to the city to escape impending danger. In the whole village of Son My that morning there were about five thousand people, only half its pre-war population because many had already fled when their hamlets first felt the ravage of bombs and bullets. Today all are gone. No one and nothing stands here anymore.

Walking north of the road, toward what used to be Xom Lang, along a muddy path winding through wild and scrubby growth which covers the once-lush rice paddies and small truck gardens, one must be careful to stay on the path. It has been marked with string and white pieces of cloth. What lies on the other side of these markers one does not know and does not risk finding out. To one side of the path there are a couple of new vegetable patches, recently trampled and crushed. The VC were hiding near here recently, using the cover to raise some food. American troops moved in, killed some, captured some and the rest fled, probably north to Batangan, still a VC sanctuary.

Just beyond these new gardens is what was Xom Lang. If one looks closely, one can count perhaps fifteen or twenty ruins. Where houses once stood, there is a rubble of bricks and cinders, covered over by rampant growth. This jungle quickly blankets everything after the monsoons and the rainy season (and there have been two since that morning) unless it is cleared away. From the rubble it is apparent that many of the houses in Xom Lang were brick, permanent structures, not the thatched "hootches" so common to less permanent, less affluent settlements. To one side there is what may have been a Buddhist pagoda. But it is now only a memory.

If one pushes away the growth, near each of what were once homes, one can see the remains of underground bunkers, shelters where the people hid from bombs and artillery shells and rockets; where some cowered all that March day hoping to avoid discovery while boots trampled overhead, emerging when the day was through into a charnel house.

A short way outside Xom Lang is a winding ditch. Now, in the rainy season, it is filled with muddy water. It is a canal, or an irrigation ditch, or a drainage ditch. Just beyond, a few hundred feet, is another. On that March morning, the two ditches were dry and dusty; the rainy season was over and the rice within a few weeks of harvest. There is no blood in the ditches now. That day they ran with blood, tears and cries.

There are craters, shell holes, gouged out of the earth all around. They are slightly eroded, no longer new. They drip with mud and water and, the debris of the Americans who have been in and out of the ruins recently. Anyone would know that Americans had been here, for it seems that we mark our passage with the garbage of our civilization—discarded cartridge shells and tin cans, empty pop bottles and ration containers, rags and scraps of paper, strew the ground.

Somewhere in here there may be booby traps and land mines. But it is impossible to know if there are or where they may be planted, and so one walks carefully, following in somebody else's tracks, walking only in fairly open, trampled areas, many of which have been marked to show that, at least a few days before, they were safe. The wild growth covers everything and makes discovery of danger unlikely without a careful sweep by mine detectors.

(Flying overhead in a helicopter later, one can get a panoramic view of the desolation. The ruins of the village, of the hamlet, of the sub-hamlets, of Xom Lang and Binh Dong and the rest, are harder to discern; one sees only desolation. But near the ruins of Xom Lang one can see three mounds as one hovers over the area; a photographer at the Americal headquarters in

Chu Lai who has made the trip with his camera later says that experts have identified them as mass graves.)

And over everything there is silence, a stillness so strange that one talks only in whispers. The only sounds are the hushed voices of Americans and, it seems, the careful and softened step of boots.

On the other side of the road from the ruins of Xom Lang, squatting at the base of Nui Da Voi—Elephant Hill—is the only place in the area of what was the village of Son My where people still live. It is the refugee camp for some of those who once lived here, and for others from villages destroyed by Americans as they tried to clear eastern Quang Ngai Province of VC. Across the entrance to the camp, in red letters on a white cloth, are the words: Khu Hoi Cu Son My, literally, gathering-place-for-the-former-Son-My-area.

This new refugee camp is surrounded by barbed concertina wire and fences of stripped and sharpened bamboo poles. It is set back a couple of hundred yards from the road and can be reached only by a narrow mud path-embankment raised above the water-filled moats which serve both as protection and as rice paddies. The camp is protected, too, by the enormous firepower available to a small, five-man squad of American Marines— called a CAP team, or a Combined Action Platoon—and a larger unit of South Vietnamese Regional Force soldiers, the Ruff-Puffs, camped alongside the refugee settlement.

The camp itself is a congerie of tin-sided-and-roofed huts on the east and, on the west, a larger mélange of hootches, the thatched-sided-and-roofed frail-looking hovels supported on a framework of bamboo poles. The floors are leveled and packed dirt; mud in the rainy season as the water flows down Elephant Hill and deluges everything. More than two thousand people crowd these huts set in rows along narrow, muddy, swamp-like

19

lanes running backward from the entrance of the camp to Elephant Hill.

We walk carefully up the twisting embankment to the entrance from the road. Just inside the bamboo fence an old man kneels, gnarled and twisted as the roots he digs painfully from the ground. We stop to talk with him for a moment. He does not cease his work, and does not look up as he talks. His name, he says, is Tran Thuoc and he is forty-four. I am surprised; he looks nearly twice that. He had been a prisoner of the ARVN for three months in 1968, suspected of VC sympathies. When he was released, he says, he returned to his hamlet of Tu Cung. Only it was not there anymore. He searched for many months until he finally found his wife in a refugee camp. She told him that the GI's had come one day and killed many people including some of his relatives. "They killed my two cows, my two buffalo," he says.

Then he looks up. "But you must see the hamlet chief. I can not talk to you more."

So we walk further into the camp, to a booth that looks like a carnival stand. Inside the booth is a young man. His name is Do Tan Nhien. He is the hamlet chief of Tu Cung, appointed and "elected" by the people—for elected officials mean more money from the government than appointed ones. He had once lived in the hamlet but had left it in 1964, when the VC arrived, and until taking this job he had worked as an ARVN cadre.

He does not want to discuss the "incident" at Xom Lang. "It was war," he tells us. Then he adds, "One of my brothers, Do Tro, his wife and two of his children, my nephews, were killed in the incident, but it is war. And I was not there, so I know nothing about it."

Are there people here who do?

"There are people in the camp from Tu Cung, yes. But you must not go back there."

Why?

"It is not safe. I have no protection that I can give you, so you must not go into the camp."

We are willing to take the risk. After all, there is a CAP team and the Regional Force group right here.

He changes his tack. "Do you have a letter from the province chief?"

What kind of a letter?

"A letter saying you may come here to see the people."

No.

"Then I cannot permit you into the camp."

I turn to the American colonel who came with us and ask whether he knows anything about the need for a letter. The colonel says he has not heard of such a thing before. This is passed on to the hamlet chief. He shakes his head. "Without a letter, I cannot let you into the camp."

Then we will go back and get a letter. It just means another trip, that's all. The colonel intervenes, and through my interpreter tells the hamlet chief that he has never heard of the need of a letter before.

The hamlet chief looks at the colonel. Then he looks back. "You should get such a letter. But, this time, I will let you into the camp without one." Then he returns to his former line. "But I have no men to accompany you. I cannot be responsible for your safety. You should not enter."

You don't have to be responsible for our safety. What can happen to us in this camp? It's protected.

"Much can happen."

For another moment he tries to block the way and then, reluctantly, steps aside. (A few days later, we would meet the hamlet chief, Do Tan Nhien, again, this time miles away outside a Buddhist pagoda in Quang Ngai. At that time, we would be talking to a woman, Nguyen Chi, whose husband was killed at

Xom Lang. During the conversation, Nhien suddenly appeared and began yelling at Nguyen Chi, telling her not to say anymore, not to talk, that she was asking for trouble. Then he stomped off, up a hill. He was, it seemed, Nguyen Chi's brother; he lived not at the Son My camp but with her at another camp, protected by the Buddhists, in Quang Ngai.)

Now we start up the hill through the muddy lanes of the camp, seeking people from Tu Cung, from Xom Lang and Binh Dong. We find one man who tells us to make it brief. The hamlet chief has warned him not to speak to Americans seeking information. "You must leave," he says, "before the hamlet chief finds I have talked with you."

As we are talking to another man, several people approach and tell those listening that they must not speak with the Americans. Seven people have been taken from the camp—all survivors of Xom Lang—for talking to Americans and all have been warned to say nothing more or they will be taken away, too. "The chief said," one man asserts, "the next time you talk you should have trouble, so shut your mouth."

So for a time, we wander about and talk in general terms with people. I have noticed in each hut a dirt bunker has been bored into the ground, usually beneath a raised wooden or dirt sleeping platform, and surrounding it are bags filled with dirt or sand. The bunkers, we are told, were built as soon as the framework for the huts had been erected. At night many people sleep under the platforms in the protected bunkers.

Why do you build the bunkers?

"To protect us from the artillery and the bombs."

But you are in a protected camp. Do you really expect to be attacked, to need such protection?

"We never know. It could come. If the shells fall, we must be ready."

Do you think the VC will send rockets into the camp?

A shrug, no emotion in the face. "It is possible. We do not know."

The look demands another question. Is it against the VC that you've built the bunkers?

Another shrug.

Who, then?

A long pause. Then, with no emotion showing in the face, "The Americans have the artillery and the planes and the choppers with bombs and rockets."

But this camp is protected by the Americans. And the ARVN, the Regional Forces are right here, too.

"Who knows. It has happened." A pause. "The RF's were here, on this hill, when the Americans came before."

And so each night, these refugees in the camp across the road from what was once a hamlet crawl into their bunkers and, in resignation and fear, wait and sleep.

During the day the people have lately begun to leave the camp, walking a short distance across the road, to attempt some reclamation of the rice paddies and vegetable gardens that have lain fallow since March of 1968. But they cultivate only those within short sight and easy run of the camp. At the slightest indication of danger or at the first sign of darkness, they trot quickly across the road and up the twisting mud embankment into camp.

We stop outside a hootch in the camp to which we have been directed, led by a young girl who once lived across the road. There has been no sense of danger in the camp yet. And now we see the hamlet chief, Nhien, coming up the lane and I smile at him. Nhien looks angry and walks past. A few moments later, about fifty feet up the hill, there is the rattle of small arms fire, a dozen shots. I look quickly around but there is nothing to see until, a moment later, there is Nhien emerging from a hootch, smiling.

So now I bend down and peer into the opening of this hootch. An old man, so thin that his arms are like peeled bamboo poles, the bones of his face stretching the skin tautly over the sharp cheekbones, sits with emotionless face and eyes on the sleeping platform inside. He is barely discernable in the dimness. He has a wispy beard that makes him look, in his frailness, not unlike Ho Chi Minh.

From Tu Cung? The question sounds loud in the low hootch.

He looks up, nods, his face solemn. Rising, he comes to the doorway and then squats in the mud. We stand outside, leaning in under the thatched overhang as protection against the steady drizzle that turns the mud into a viscous river. All around children have gathered, giggling, laughing, pointing, approaching and suddenly pulling the hair on my arms.

"The earth, the sky, the sea, they were all good to us," the old man says in a sing-songy voice. He does not raise his eyes or turn his head to look down the lane, across the road toward the desolation where his home had once been. "But," he says after a while, "Horse Mountain crossed the river."

Buried somewhere in antiquity is the day when the first of the Nam Viets, as these people were then called, arrived in this corner of the Asian world. More than 2,500 years ago they fled from southern China to escape the rule of the Chinese, and the assimilative pressures of the expanding empire. Slowly they moved south, across the Red River and, as the Chinese continued to push behind them, continued their southward migration.

Eventually the first of them arrived at this bulge in the Southeast Asian peninsula along the coast of the South China Sea in what would, centuries later, be called the province of Quang Ngai in the southern half of the Kingdom of Annam, one of the three parts of Vietnam. Today it is divided roughly in half, one part in North Vietnam, the other in South Vietnam. The other two parts are: Tonkin, in what is now the Democratic Republic of Vietnam, or North Vietnam; and Cochinchina in the tropical jungles of the south, in South Vietnam.

Those who decided to stay here must have thought that China was far enough away to the north (though the Chinese would eventually overrun even this area and impose a suzerainty that lasted, off and on, for centuries). Nowhere would they find a more ideal spot. The sea was filled with fish, easily caught. The low lands, drained and washed by the Cho Mai and the other rivers to the north, by the Tra Khuc to the south, and by myriad streams in between, were ideal for growing rice and vegetables, for grazing buffalo. And except for the rainy season and the floods of late fall and early winter—and they were necessary if the rice were to grow—the weather was almost always warm and pleasant.

So some stopped and built their homes and their villages. With all that was necessary for sustenance around them and, they thought, effectively protected and isolated by the rivers north and south and by the sea on the east, they lived to themselves, unconcerned with the world outside their villages. Content, they were most of the time unaware even of what was happening as close as the next village across the river. "That village," one would say, and the people still say it today, "was two *klick* [two kilometers] from my hamlet, so I did not know what was happening there." They had all they needed and their needs were not many. So they found no cause to worry about events outside their immediate neighborhood as long as the events did not encroach upon them.

"We have always been here," a village elder from Son My says, sitting in a refugee camp on the edge of Quang Ngai, but motioning eastward with his hand. Those gathered around him, listening attentively to the conversation, always ready to break in to amplify a point or correct what they consider an error, nod in agreement. "This was the home of our ancestors. There was no need for them to leave and no reason for them to think about events somewhere else. There was no need for most of us to leave. Until now. But some of us will not ever leave. This is our home. We wait only for the day we can return."

Four villages gradually came into being over the centuries in this region along the coast. Because of their contiguousness and because of the natural borders sealing them from the outside, there was a blending of the villages. They traded with each other, sometimes they marketed their rice and fish mutually, and there were marriages and social contacts between them. But all four still attempted to maintain their own distinctive identities even though many from the outside considered them in essence a single village. Eventually they would become in fact a single village called Son My. But that would not happen until 1945.

The four villages, of an equal size and of a similar population (by the middle of the twentieth century, before the ravages of war struck them, each would contain about twenty-five hundred people) were called My Lai, Co Luy, My Khe and Tu Cung. My Lai was along the coast to the northeast; just below it on the coast was Co Luy; inland and west of Co Luy was My Khe; and north of My Khe, west of My Lai, was Tu Cung.

"This," a provincial official in Quang Ngai city says, pointing to a map of the province and referring to the whole area and not to any one of the four villages as distinct from the others, "was the most beautiful village in all of Quang Ngai, maybe in all of Vietnam. You should have seen in the old days the beautiful fields and the beaches and the houses. It was famous for its beauty."

Many settlements in Vietnam, particularly in the jungles of the south and in the barrenness of the mountains to the west, had houses that were but frail, impermanent hootches, and inhabitants who seemed willing in bad times to abandon their villages and move to places, a few miles away, where things might prove

26

a little better. These villages of Son My, however, were embedded in the earth and part of the intrinsic character of the land. The people settled down, fished and farmed, raised their families and, in good times, prospered. As the children grew and married and began to farm their own paddies farther away from the original hamlets, new hamlets sprang up, though remaining under the roof of the village of their fathers. And over the years the original thatched houses began to vanish, replaced by new homes made of brick with thatched roofs, homes with more than a single room, homes with wood or brick rather than packed dirt floors. About these four villages there was the aura of permanence and prosperity.

The reputation for beauty and serenity spread gradually beyond the immediate realm of the villages. Late in the nineteenth century a native son of Tu Cung named Truong Dang Que ventured from his village into the world. He won a place for himself in the court of King Tu Duc, eventually rising to become one of the King's most important ministers. According to the stories told by the villagers, Que boasted continuously to the King and the court of the wonders of Tu Cung. Eventually, as a reward for his services, the King gave him an order to build a villa for himself at Tu Cung, and then provided him with the funds to build it.

When Que died, his son took his father's place in the confidences of the King and court, and continued his constant talk of home. Such talk had the same effect as the myths of El Dorado on the Spanish. Over the years, some of the ministers made the pilgrimage seeking the wonders of the region, found them to be true and built summer villas for themselves along the rivers and on the shore where the beaches were broad and golden and, except in rainy winter, the weather mild and ideal.

The French came, too. For about this time, the French extended their colonial empire to incorporate what they called

27

Indochina—the three parts of Vietnam as well as Laos and Cambodia. Wealthy Vietnamese still vacationed in the four villages and, after a time, they were joined by some of the French colonial officials from Hue and Da Nang and Quang Ngai, and from cities even farther away, north and south. Even the Vietnamese working in Quang Ngai as government functionaries, clerks or merchants, with a little extra money and a little extra time, began to make the short trip from the city to the beach on Sundays or, if they had relatives living in one of the four villages and thus had a place to stay, for the entire weekend.

The arrival of vacationers and weekend guests meant only a little more prosperity for the people of the villages. The visitors came and left money, though the wealthy Vietnamese and the French stayed pretty much to themselves, dealing with the local residents only when absolutely necessary. And the local people, when they could, ignored their visitors, devoting themselves as they always had to fishing and rice growing, building stronger and more permanent houses. Their prosperity enabled them not only to have better things for themselves, for their homes and better equipment for their work, but it permitted them to build a high school near the boundary between Tu Cung and My Lai villages so that literacy was at a high level. And with such literacy, added to their contacts with the outside, they developed at least a limited degree of political and social sophistication. Enough, anyway, to be aware of and disturbed by the corruption and inefficiency among the agents of the government who came to collect taxes from them, to tell them about the government and to attempt to give them orders.

For the most part, though, they resisted efforts by the world outside to encroach and to bring change. They maintained their independence and their pride, more determined than ever from all they saw to hold it tightly, to be left alone.

Besides, many were sure that things were never going to

change very much for them, that the world would leave them alone to live their lives as lives had always been lived in the villages, though perhaps just a little better. For in the southern part of My Khe village, near the Tra Khuc River, stood the tallest hill in the area, Nui Ngura, or Horse Mountain. And there was an ancient saying: "When Horse Mountain crosses the river, our village will know no more law and no more peace." Whoever heard of a mountain crossing a river?

But change came. First the French were uprooted as the Japanese arrived to rule Indochina during World War II. Though late in the war some of the young men from the villages went off to join the Viet Minh and the other resistance movements fighting the Japanese, this change in faraway rulers really meant very little to the people of the four villages. The tax collectors, if different individuals, were nevertheless still Vietnamese. They just happened to be working for the Japanese now rather than the French. But the taxes remained just about the same, and the Japanese themselves were not often seen in this far off corner of the world. The people paid, grumbled about the corruption of the officials who always seemed desirous of bribes from the rich, and went about their work, still isolated from the rest of the world and unconcerned about it as long as they were left to themselves.

Then the war was over. But the French did not immediately return. Quang Ngai became a center of the Viet Minh strength, both in 1945 when the Viet Minh proclaimed itself the government of the nation of Vietnam and later when the war between the French and the Viet Minh broke out. One of the major Viet Minh leaders, Pham Van Dong, later to become Prime Minister of North Vietnam, was born and grew up in Quang Ngai, south of the four villages. In the province, Pham Van Dong and Ho Chi Minh were both hailed as heroes and patriots.

Change was at hand. The Viet Minh controlled the area, and

worked to solidify its support among the people, or at least to win a favorable neutrality, (which is about the best that anyone can hope for from most of these normally uncommitted peasants) by fostering positive changes.

The tax collectors were no longer amenable to bribes; they were honest and went about their work diligently; if they favored anyone, it was the poor man over the rich man. This was a radical shift from the past.

Some of the land that had belonged to absentee landlords was redistributed. Some of the young men, won by the dream of independence for the whole nation as well as for their villages and swayed by what seemed the honesty and incorruptibility of the Viet Minh with whom they dealt, joined the revolt. Some left home to fight in Ho's army; some stayed to work as Viet Minh cadre and what came to be called infra-structure among their own people in their own villages.

And then the four villages became one.

For the Viet Minh administrators, there was no logic in having four villages in what was basically a single geographic entity. It was like saying that the parts of a water buffalo are separate and have their own existences and are not part of a whole. The only logic in the present structure was ancient tradition. And such ideas can be tampered with only with extreme caution or the results could be catastrophic—loss of support, a turn from favorable neutrality to outright hostility or even resistance. Ngo Dinh Diem and his brother Ngo Dinh Nhu learned this all too well when they attempted to destroy local traditions and set up the so-called "strategic hamlets."

But in the case of these four villages (and of many others similarly situated in the province and in the country), the new organization would not really tamper with tradition. The people of the four villages had been intermingled for centuries and in fact if not in name they had long been one.

The logic on the side of the creation of a single village out of the four was simple. It would make the area easier to rule and control. Instead of having to deal with four village chiefs and their multiplicity of problems, there would be only one chief. This would simplify matters considerably. It would make for more efficient administration, simpler procedures for collection of taxes, and would centralize control and responsibility.

So the village of Son My was created in 1945 by the Viet Minh. Within its boundaries it combined what had been the four villages of My Lai, Co Luy, My Khe and Tu Cung. These four were downgraded to the status of hamlets. And the hamlets within them became sub-hamlets. While this was merely a re-shuffling for administrative reasons by the Viet Minh, it was continued after the war was over. Later, when the Americans arrived, it was to lead to bafflement and, eventually, in March of 1968, to tragedy.

Most Americans, including Americans serving with the military in Vietnam, seem to have little comprehension of what the Vietnamese mean when they talk about villages and hamlets and sub-hamlets. Perhaps we should pause here for a moment and discuss just what these terms mean.

A Vietnamese village is *not* what a village is in the United States or in Europe. It is *not* a collection of houses or a small settlement where a few people live. Rather, a village in Vietnam is a New England township or a county or a borough in micro-cosm (and, itself, the village falls within a district which most Americans would consider the county structure; thus Son My is part of the Son Tinh district).

Within the village there are smaller sub-divisions, called hamlets. Once these were the settlements where the people lived. But when the Viet Minh turned what had been villages into hamlets, these hamlets became only smaller administrative units within the larger new village. They were not collections of homes.

Where the people lived, where their homes were, were the sub-hamlets of each hamlet. Each had its own distinctive name, not the name of the larger hamlet. Before the Viet Minh changes, of course, they had been the hamlets; now they were sub-hamlets.

Thus the new village of Son My contained four hamlets: My Lai, Co Luy, My Khe and Tu Cung. Within these four hamlets there were twenty sub-hamlets and it was in them that the people resided. The hamlet of My Lai had four sub-hamlets. None was called My Lai (despite the American maps). The largest was called My Khe, the same name as the larger hamlet to the southwest and thus a name which could cause Americans, if not Vietnamese who understand such things, considerable confusions. The other sub-hamlets were Kho Truong, Dong De and Con Thieu. On the American military maps, My Khe and Kho Truong were lumped together, colored pink and, their true names ignored, labeled My Lai (1). The other two sub-hamlets were labeled My Lai (2) and My Lai (3).

Co Luy hamlet had five sub-hamlets. None was called Co Luy. They were My Hoi, My Xuan, Xuan Duong, Xuan Tung and Xuan Cua. On the American military maps, drawn on the basis of new surveys after the American involvement, these names were ignored. New names were selected by the American map-makers based either on the whole hamlet or on nearby hamlets. The names, of course, were not those by which the Vietnamese knew these settlements. Thus the five sub-hamlets of Co Luy were called My Khe (2), My Khe (4), Co Luy (1), Co Luy (2) and Co Luy (3).

My Khe hamlet had six sub-hamlets. None was called My Khe. They were Cuong Dinh, Dinh Denh, Cay Quen, An Thoi, Dong Rang and Xon Be. None of these names appeared on the American military maps. In fact, the maps ignored the existence of some and lumped others together. Thus in My Khe the

Americans noted only three settlements which they identified as My Khe (1), My Khe (2) and An Loc (1).

Tu Cung hamlet had five sub-hamlets. None was called Tu Cung. They were Xom Lang, also known as Thuan Yen, Phung Hoa, Binh Dong, Binh Tay and Thuong An. Again, these names were ignored in the preparation of the American maps; and so was the name of the whole hamlet, Tu Cung. The five sub-hamlets of Tu Cung became three for the Americans: My Lai (4)—which is Xom Lang, the scene of the initial strike on March 16, 1968—My Lai (5) and My Lai (6).

If the structure of the Vietnamese countryside—with its villages, hamlets and sub-hamlets—initially sounds confusing, it may be only because of western unfamiliarity with Vietnamese terms and names.

If we can draw an analogy, though certainly not an exact one, between a Vietnamese village and an American county—the village, of course, would be a reflection in microcosm—then perhaps it will be even clearer.

Take, say, Westchester County in New York. Within Westchester there is no distinct place called Westchester; it is the name of the whole area. Thus, Son My. Westchester includes the beaches of Long Island Sound, the Hudson River shoreline, the farming areas in the north, larger subdivisions encompassing several townships and then the populated cities, villages and towns. Again, Son My and all that was within its borders.

When one talks about Westchester County, one talks about all of it, not about a specific part of it. So, too, with Son My village. If one wants to talk about a specific part, he talks about southern Westchester or northern Westchester or the Hudson River side or the Long Island side. Thus, in Son My, one would talk about My Lai, or Tu Cung or one of the other hamlets. But if one wanted to discuss a specific town or city in Westchester, he would call it by name—New Rochelle, Bedford, Scarsdale,

Yonkers, Pleasantville. Again, in Son My if one wanted to talk to the people about a specific settlement he would call it by its name if he wished to be understood—Xom Lang, My Khe, My Hoi.

What one would not do is what American map-makers did; that is, to ignore the real names and give generalized names with numbers after them. Would an American unfamiliar with a new map with its own nomenclature know where a place called Hastings (5) or White Plains (3) or Mount Vernon (2) was? No more would he than would a Vietnamese asked were My Lai (4) or My Khe (3) was.

This, then, is part—but only part—of the American error in Vietnam. Have we gone to the right place? The Vietnamese said the VC were in My Lai, but there are six of them on our maps. Which one is the right one? How can we be sure? Is this particular spot, marked Something (1) on the map, inhabited by friends, foes or neutrals? We know the enemy is at Somewhere, but is this the right Somewhere?

If the Viet Minh, then, created a new village called Son My out of four older, smaller ones, they made few other changes that really altered the course of the people's lives. So nobody thought much about it. They lived much as they always had. And in this spot on the sea, controlled though it was by the Viet Minh, the war was still far away. There was not much fighting in the general vicinity during the Viet Minh struggle with the French, and so nothing really intruded.

With the Geneva Agreements of 1954, the war came to an end. Peace returned, though it was not much different for the people of Son My from war. The demarcation line between North and South Vietnam was drawn at the Seventeenth Parallel, about a hundred miles to the north. In the weeks before the official establishment of the two countries, those on either side of the new border were permitted to cross in either direction as their political sympathies dictated. Perhaps ten times as many Vietnamese made the trip from north to south, despite an almost national veneration for "Uncle Ho," as made the trip from the south to the north. Among those moving south, it must be remembered, were large numbers of Catholics—for Catholicism had been very strong in the north since the seventeenth century—fearful, with reason, of repressions under Communist rule.

A number of Viet Minh supporters, on the other hand, made the trip the other way. Among them were some from the sub-hamlets of Son My. They journeyed to the land of Ho and Dong to build a new life for themselves under the government they had fought for. From Xom Lang, five or six families disappeared one day, heading north, and they were joined by a few of the young men. From My Khe, a dozen or more made the trek, and about the same number left An Thoi. And so, in all the sub-hamlets throughout the village, there were for a time empty houses and young men, sometimes whole families, gone from their ancient homes to the north.

There was peace for the next few years. The crops grew, the fish filled the nets, the vacationers—almost all Vietnamese now —came again to the beaches. In the winter the rains came and the rivers filled, overflowed their banks. There were some who noticed with a touch of concern that the Tra Khuc, just as many other rivers, seemed to be changing its course slightly with each flood, edging closer to Horse Mountain. But not many gave this much thought.

It was a time of prosperity again. The days of war and trouble during the Viet Minh revolt began to fade from the mind— those days in which the thought, like some boil that has not yet erupted through the skin but nevertheless can be sensed, that the war might someday strike at Son My was at the edge of the consciousness. Even thoughts of those who had gone north

35

receded. If there were still communists, still Viet Minh, living in the sub-hamlets, they kept a silent counsel for a later day and went about their work as farmers or fishermen.

But it was not long before there were signs that trouble would come, if not immediately to Son My then at least to the country, and undoubtedly if it came it would erupt in Quang Ngai where the residue of strong Viet Minh sympathy was waiting to be stirred and quickened again.

The tax collectors came from Saigon, from the new Viet-namese government of Ngo Dinh Diem. But they were not what the tax collectors of the Viet Minh had been. These new assessors could be easily bribed by those who had the money and the burden of paying taxes fell more heavily on the poor and those in the middle. Once again, the other government officials could be swayed by bribes and influence to render decisions favorable to the rich and not the poor. Official corruption had made its reappearance and some of the people began to grumble that maybe the Viet Minh, the communists, had not been so bad after all.

Though the official policy of the Diem regime was land reform and some redistribution of land was actually carried out in scattered parts of Vietnam, the people at this corner of Quang Ngai did not see evidence of it in practice. Instead, some of the old landowners returned and with official help reclaimed their old homes and their old fields, and those who had farmed them again became landless and were forced either to rent land from the rich or to become laborers working on the land of others for hire. Their complaints were ignored, as were most complaints directed at the rich, at officials, at graft and corruption. It seemed that at least some of the hamlet chiefs and sub-hamlet chiefs, some of the members of the village and hamlet councils, had open palms when the rich came to them, and so the poor could not sway them, could not even get them to listen.

If there was cause, even in this isolated spot, for disaffection right at hand, there was additional cause in the world outside the village. The village, despite its desire for isolation and its determination to be isolated, was not totally oblivious to what was happening beyond its borders, nor was it totally unaffected by such events. There were stories transmitted by relatives who had left in the past to settle in the cities. From Hue and Saigon and the other metropolitan centers came the tales of repressions wrought by the Diem regime against political opponents and dissenters, of the government's ultra-Catholicism and its harassment of Buddhists. These people in the village were Buddhists and so they heard such stories with resentment and with growing bitterness.

Further, there was evidence closer at hand of the regime's methods and practices, evidence which further enhanced the disenchantment. There was what was happening in Quang Ngai city, in the whole province and in the northern area of Vietnam of which the province was a part. For this northern district was the purview of two of Diem's brothers, Archbishop Ngo Dinh Thuc and Ngo Dinh Can.

Thuc was the spiritual leader of the region's Catholics, and he preached constantly that Catholicism could survive in Vietnam only as a militant, permanent crusade. Many interpreted this to mean that non-believers would be crushed. There were enough tales of attacks on the Buddhists, the repressive measures leveled against the bonzes, to lend credence to this belief.

The political ruler of the northern region was Can, who spoke with his presidential brother's voice and was considered by many even crueler and more vindictive than the fourth and perhaps most powerful of the Ngo brothers, Ngo Dinh Nhu. So hated were the two brothers in the region they controlled with ungloved steel fists that they were rarely seen in public once the Viet Cong surfaced. Archbishop Thuc when he left Hue toured

37

the provinces in an armored car with an armed military escort. Can was constantly surrounded by armed body guards. And the dicta that emerged from them more and more alienated the Buddhist majority, alienated those who professed only neutrality and a desire to be left alone.

Eventually after the fall of the Diem regime in November of 1963, the people of Hue were prepared to seize and burn both Thuc and Can at the stake. Thuc, however, had been called to Rome shortly before; he had earned papal displeasure and was being removed in fact if not in name, from his jurisdiction. Thus he was saved. Not so fortunate was Can. He took refuge with the American consul. But six months later, the Americans turned him over to the new government in Saigon. He was tried and publicly executed.

The Diem regime, then, was planting the seeds of revolt and of its own destruction in soil which was fertile, where they would grow rapidly and multiply.

The trouble began in a small way, with the emergence of a guerrilla band—the rebirth of the Viet Minh as what would soon be called the Viet Cong—in the mountains of western Quang Ngai Province late in 1959. It was soon joined by other small guerrilla bands operating in the Mekong Delta in the south and in other areas around the country. In December, 1960, with the revolt in full movement, political leadership arrived. That month, at some isolated spot in what had been Cochinchina, the National Liberation Front, the political arm of the Viet Cong, was born. The war had begun which would soon embroil the whole country and eventually lead to turning much of it into a desert.

But the Vietnamese peasants, both in these early days and later, unless they were directly in the line of fire, viewed the VC, the NLF, the government and the whole struggle, with a degree of detachment. The Vietnamese are an old and, in many ways, cynical and sophisticated people. Through the centuries they have seen governments come and go. They have seen foreign invaders hold sway for a time, to be replaced by other foreign rulers, or, perhaps, by some local mandarin, or, on rare occasions, by a more national regime in Hue, Saigon or Hanoi. They had heard the calls, by this leader or that one, to rally to the cause of national unity almost since they had arrived in this southern peninsula. But such unity, linking the whole country from the borders of China to Cape Ca Mau at the southern tip, had been achieved for only about thirty years in all Vietnamese history. Thus the calls were greeted with more than a little skepticism and a reluctance to throw in with, or against, the side issuing them.

And with the experience of the ages, the Vietnamese peasants had come to believe that there was only a difference of degree, not of kind, between almost all who had ruled them. Except for a natural desire to be ruled, if one must be ruled at all (and the farther away the rulers, the better), by one's own people rather than some outsiders, there was little reason for the peasants to choose sides. Especially as in most cases, they were not really forced to make a choice.

"Until the Americans came," said one old man in a refugee camp near Quang Ngai, "whoever was the government, whoever ruled our village, the French, the Japanese, the Viet Minh, Saigon, the VC, it did not matter. They would come to our hamlet and collect their taxes. Sometimes they would lecture us, tell us what they were doing for us, how they were protecting us from trouble on the outside so that we could continue to live in peace. Sometimes they would listen to our complaints, though they usually did nothing about them. Sometimes they would take our young men to be soldiers, to fight in their wars. But then they would leave, and we would be alone again to do as we had always done, to farm, to raise our children."

With all their grievances, real and imagined, against the government in Saigon and the Ngo family, the people of Son My and of many other villages all over Vietnam tried to remain aloof from the struggle erupting around them. They did little but grumble at the government. They were cerain that this government, like all those others down through the centuries, would eventually give way to another, and whether of the military or the VC or someone else, this new government would be different only in degree. No matter who was in control, they were convinced, their lives basically would remain as they always had. As long as neither the Saigon government nor the VC interfered with them overly much, they would maintain that same kind of neutrality they had shown to all governments and all rebels in the past, and wait.

There were, of course, many who were not prepared to wait and who planned and knew how to use the grievances of the peasants for their own devices, how to mobilize them against the government. They were waiting, the Viet Cong and the National Liberation Front, the communists.

Once they surfaced in 1959 and 1960, they fed the hungry maw of discontent with no little success. There were the real afflictions of the people, both in the cities and in the countryside. There were the minor grievances which could be made to seem larger and more important. There was the still-remembered support that had existed for the Viet Minh in its struggle against the French and the veneration with which many still viewed Ho Chi Minh; he was the national patriot and, especially to the poor and landless, he was the promise of an end to their misery. There were the terror tactics which the VC used often to control and intimidate the population or, at least, to confirm a neutrality among the people.

And there were the growing and extreme counter-measures adopted by Diem and Nhu in their fight with the Viet Cong—

the repressions of the Buddhists, the total disruption and destruction of rural tradition with the "strategic hamlet" concept which forceably moved people from their ancient homes to new "protected" resettlement camps.

But in these years of the early 1960's, for most Vietnamese the war was still far away, something rumored but not seen. There were areas, of course, where battles erupted, where the VC and the government were in constant contention. But only the people in those areas were directly affected, and they were a small minority of the population. For the majority, there was little appreciable alteration in the unchanging pattern of life. If they lived in an area controlled by the government, they lived as they had lived since the partition and as they had lived long before it. If they were in an area taken over by the VC which the government was not at that point prepared to contest, for most this meant only a change of masters; most of those who objected to the change left for government-controlled ground.

The Americans, with all their vast firepower, which would mean a vast expansion of the war, had not yet arrived in massive numbers. That would not happen until 1965 and after.

Son My was in an area under government control during those first years of the VC insurrection. In the village and in much of Quang Ngai along the coast (though not in the mountainous interior), the VC were still dormant, waiting. And so the people of the village were able to live and act almost as though there was no war.

But in the winter of 1963–1964, Horse Mountain crossed the river.

The rains started early that winter, fell harder than usual, and the rivers rose higher and higher. They poured over their banks and the floods rolled across the land. The road from the coast inland was inundated. Son My was isolated completely from Quang Ngai city and the protection of the government troops.

There was no way to get through to the city for those who might have wanted to get through; even the trip by boat was risky along the flooded Tra Khuc River.

In the southern part of the village, in My Khe hamlet, the fulfillment of the ancient prophecy was at hand. The waters of the Tra Khuc rose higher and spilled across their banks, lapping at the base of Horse Mountain. As the floods continued, the water climbed higher on the hill and seeped around it. Horse Mountain was in the midst of the waters, an island. Those who saw it, as the rains stopped, were stricken. Horse Mountain had crossed the river.

And when the floods finally receded, the Tra Khuc had once again carved a slightly new channel for itself. With the change, it had cut away part of Horse Mountain.

The news quickly spread through the village. There was trepidation, especially among the old, and a conviction that it would not be long before the rest of the prophecy worked itself out.

The rains had stopped but the flood waters were still high. Le Quang Hai, then fifty-five and the hamlet chief of My Lai hamlet, came out of his house in My Khe sub-hamlet one morning early in 1964. He remembers that he saw a group of men standing in the center of My Khe, waiting patiently. Hai stared at them uncertainly, wondering how they had gotten to My Khe with the flood waters still on the land. He wondered who they could be, though the longer he stared at them the more familiar they seemed. Then he recognized them, though they were older than when he had last seen them ten years before. They were some of the men who had gone north, to North Vietnam, in 1954. Now they had returned. The VC had arrived to take control of Son My village.

In all the sub-hamlets that morning and on succeeding mornings, three or four men who had gone north a decade before made their re-appearance, and an almost forgotten and dead flame was quickened. These were not strangers, as were many of the officials often sent by the Saigon government to deal with the people in the village. These were old neighbors, old friends. Perhaps in those dim years one had argued with them about politics, about leaving home. But they were neighbors and friends, nevertheless.

They had returned with a message. They were taking command of the village. With them they had weapons to enforce their desires, if that were necessary. And they had support as well, from those relatives they had left behind and from those VC supporters who had lain dormant all the years.

They had little difficulty in assuming control. The area was effectively sealed from the outside and so there was really no one with the power to dispute them. What had to be done before the floods receded was to solidify that control. The VC returnees did that quickly and almost effortlessly. After all, they had the power in their weapons, in the support of their relatives and the silent VC cadre, and they had it by playing on the grievances of the people, especially the poor and those in the middle.

Within a couple of days, the members of the village council—the ruling body—and the hamlet and sub-hamlet councils were arrested and brought to trial before a specially convened "People's Court," composed of representatives of the poor and the whole hamlet wherever a trial was held.

As one former deputy hamlet chief in one of Son My's hamlets describes it, the twelve members of his hamlet council, including himself, were seized by the VC, their former neighbors, and brought before the court one evening.

"They accused us," he says, "of having worked for the *nguy chinh phu*—the 'puppet government'—in Saigon. They accused us of having favored the rich against the poor. They accused us of having taken bribes and graft and on and on. I was afraid. Everyone was afraid. We thought we would all be killed by the VC, for we had been told by the government that such would happen if the VC came to our village and took command. But some of the people from my hamlet got up in the court and they told the VC that although I had worked for the government in Saigon, I was a good man. I had treated them well. I had never taken a bribe. I was fair to the people, and so and so. That I was a good guy."

What happened?

"The VC listened to the people. They took me to the north, to a training school where they indoctrinated me in communism, in their revolution."

Then?

"They sent me back to the hamlet. But when I got back to my hamlet, I ran away and came here, to Quang Ngai, for safety."

Why?

"I did not like all that they said in the north. And with the VC here, I knew that my hamlet would not be safe. Someday, the ARVN or the Americans would come and then there would be a battle and many people would be killed. So I left before that could happen."

What happened to the other members of the hamlet council? Did the VC kill them?

"No. The VC killed no one in my hamlet. Some of them they arrested and took to the jungle. They have not returned, so maybe the VC did kill them there. But they did not kill them in the hamlet."

And the others?

"Some they forced to leave the hamlet, to leave all of Son My. The VC told them not to come back. Others they made laborers, to work in the fields, to build roads, to dig tunnels, to carry supplies, to do all kinds of work for the VC. But these were men the people in the hamlet opposed. Others, whom the people spoke for, the VC did nothing to."

After the trials, nobody doubted that the VC were indeed in control of Son My. They appointed new hamlet and village chiefs and councils, those who were loyal to them or at least were neutral but leaning in their direction. They made certain, though, that these new officials were not men who were anathema to the people but men who had at least some support and were respected as honest and capable.

In control, the VC explained what the future would hold for Son My.

The village was cut off from the government by the flood. When the rivers returned to their normal level and the land dried, the government would find that it could not return. The VC would control the road from just past the old citadel at Chau Thanh to the sea. This was the only land access to Son My and anyone trying to use it could be stopped by the VC lying in ambush if that were the VC's desire. The VC, thus, would have dominion over who came to Son My and who left it.

However, it was made clear, the village would not be totally isolated. The people could go to market as they always had, trade with those they had always traded with and continue to deal with the interior in a nearly normal fashion. And many people would be permitted to journey into the village from the interior, from Quang Ngai. The VC might even permit some officials from the government to come to the village on occasion. But it would be known to all that this was territory under VC control, that those who traveled in it did so with the VC's sufferance and that at any time without any warning the VC could, to prove its supremacy, stop all traffic.

If this was now to be a VC realm, the VC, however, would not keep anyone within it under duress. Those who wanted to leave for good and live with the government could do so. But if they left, they could take nothing with them. Everything would be left behind to belong to the hamlet and to be used for the whole hamlet, and this included any land.

Many of those who could leave did leave. "The rich, those who had relatives on the outside or who had money on the outside, they left when the VC arrived," an official in the provincial office in Quang Ngai explained. He himself had originally come from Xom Lang though he had left it many years before; some of his relatives followed him to the city when the VC took over; some stayed behind, some later to die, though not at the hands of the VC. "Those who stayed in Xom Lang and in the other places," he said, "they were mainly the poor people or the sympathizers of the VC. But the majority of the people were not rich. So they could not leave. And if they stayed, they had to cooperate with the VC."

Those who stayed soon learned, both from the VC and by experience, that there would be no trouble from the VC if they cooperated. They might actually be better off than they had been (as long as the Americans and the ARVN did not actively contest the VC's control). The lands of absentee landlords and of those who left were turned over to the hamlet councils and many of the landless were able to rent paddies at low prices; if they had the money, they could even buy them with the funds going into a hamlet treasury for the benefit of all.

Some of the money, of course, went to pay a VC war tax. The people now paid their taxes directly to the VC and not to Saigon. These taxes, in the form of rice for the most part, were collected twice a year—in late March and August, after the rice harvests. Taxes from the fishermen were collected more often, though they did not come to more than the taxes on the rice farmers. The tax rate was a progressive one, based on the amount of rice each family grew. For those in the middle, the tax averaged out to about a third of the harvest; the poor, with little land and just about enough to feed their families, paid nothing; the rich paid much more. For an average farmer, then, the tax amounted to about four hundred litres of rice, while for the rich it could reach a thousand litres.

The richest man in Xom Lang when the VC arrived was a man everyone called Mr. Sam. With his wealth in his rice fields and with many relatives to take care of and as head of his family name, Mr. Sam decided to remain in the hamlet even though he opposed the VC. The VC permitted him to do as he had always done as long as he paid his taxes and did not interfere with them. His tax was set at a thousand litres of rice. If he refused to pay, he was told and he knew, it would mean reprisal.

But within a year after the VC's arrival, Mr. Sam found that it would leave him in dire straits if he paid what the VC asked after one harvest. When he refused to pay, he was arrested and taken off to the jungle and a VC prison camp.

About four months after his arrest, Mr. Sam returned to Xom Lang. He had managed to escape from the prison and work his way back home through jungle trails and mountains. The VC in the sub-hamlet made no comment when he reappeared. He moved back into his house with his family, assumed control of his land once again. But he never again raised any objection to paying the taxes set for him by the VC. Though he never told anyone what had happened to him in the jungle prison, refused to discuss it with anyone, he made it plain that such an experience was to be avoided if at all possible.

The people—including Mr. Sam—found that these taxes, and several special war taxes which were assessed from time to time, were collected honestly and efficiently and equitably. This was stressed by the VC and demonstrated by the collectors. The people were warned that any attempt to bribe or corrupt an official would be dealt with severely. Just how severely was never spelled out, but with the example of Mr. Sam before them

47

for refusal to pay taxes and not for what was considered the greater crime of attempted corruption or bribery, the people thought they had a pretty good idea. And honest officials, even if VC, were welcomed by most of the people in Son My after their experiences with the Saigon functionaries who were not merely easily bribable but seemed to want to be bribed.

By such a mixture of threats and promises, punishments and rewards, the VC were able to rule the hamlet with little opposition—especially since there were no troops around initially to turn the area into a battleground and thereby make the people bitter at the VC for bringing death and destruction to them.

What the VC expected, in very basic terms, was soon apparent in Son My, as it was apparent wherever the VC took command. The people were expected to provide shelter when needed. In general practice, though, the VC, when present in any large numbers—and this was true usually only in My Khe sub-hamlet of My Lai—would take over abandoned homes or spend their days in bunkers and tunnels, emerging only at night. And often the VC were gone entirely, off on guerrilla missions somewhere in the province or even farther away, leaving behind only the small VC infra-structure to hold sway.

The villagers were expected to volunteer for any kind of job the VC wanted done—picking rocks from fields, building hidden roads, making and laying bricks, constructing tunnels and bunkers, building booby traps, planting land mines, acting as weapons and supply carriers when a VC patrol went into the field.

Says one refugee from Son My who remained in his hamlet all through the VC period, "When the people, especially the rich people, but still all the people, knew that the VC wanted something done, they knew they must volunteer first, before the VC came and chose them, those who do so and so. They feared that if they did not volunteer, the VC might arrest them.

So usually anyone who had worked for Saigon in the past, he must volunteer first for anything the VC wanted."

The VC, of course, wanted recruits as much as anything else. For the young men in the hamlets, those in their late teens—above sixteen—and those in their early twenties who were not married and did not have children, there was always the danger that they would be selected in a VC draft. So they had to choose between several alternatives: they could stay at home in their hamlet and when the VC started a recruitment drive, become a VC soldier; they could stay in their hamlet and when the VC started a recruitment drive, flee to the city and become an ARVN soldier: they could leave immediately for the city and either become ARVN or try to disappear into the crowd. Some did one thing, some another. And there were a number of families in the hamlets and sub-hamlets of Son My who had sons fighting for the VC and other sons fighting with the ARVN, and many who had other relatives with both the VC and the ARVN.

Mr. Sam, for example, had a nephew who was drafted by the VC soon after they took control. One of his sons married a girl from Xom Lang named Ngo Ngo Thininh when both were eighteen. Before she became pregnant, the VC began a recruiting drive. The young husband fled the village and joined the ARVN in Quang Ngai. He was, thus, on one side while his cousin was on the other but his father, his wife, his uncle and most of his other relatives, like most of the people, tried to play at some sort of forced cooperative neutrality.

Whatever the VC wanted done was usually done, since there were some VC—either soldiers or infra-structure—always around to make sure that their desires were filled. In each of the sub-hamlets there were some VC, usually only two or three. Except, again, at My Khe, where elements of the VC's 48th Local Force Battalion were often present in some force.

At night, at irregular intervals save at tax collecting times, there would be visits from local VC officials and sometimes from representatives of the far-off National Liberation Front.

These officials would usually come into a sub-hamlet about dusk, accompanied proudly by the local VC activists and sympathizers. But unlike the Saigon government men who used to arrive, the VC would have a thorough understanding of what was going on in the sub-hamlet—who was arguing with whom over what, who thought his neighbor was cheating him, who was talking aloud against the VC, who was actively cooperating, who had legitimate complaints that should be dealt with quickly. They had been briefed in advance, and well-briefed, by their allies on local conditions.

On the evenings where these visiting officials were to put in an appearance, the sub-hamlet VC would round up much of the population and gather it in a central spot for the meeting. Generally, there was not much hesitation on the part of these peasants when the call came. After all, the meetings were a break in the unchanging day-to-day existence and there were not just speeches but entertainment as well.

If anyone did object, as was sometimes Mr. Sam's wont, he was not forced to attend. He was permitted to stay at home or, if he had already arrived at the meeting place, was permitted to return to his home, sometimes even escorted politely by VC.

Pham Phon is another who says that he did not ever go to the meetings of the VC. A forty-eight-year-old farmer who owned no land of his own and rented a small plot from the village where he grew rice, he says, "The VC used to come at night to round up the people for their meetings. They would knock at the doors and tell the people to gather. But I dared not meet them. I was afraid. I locked my door and would not look at them. I would not answer the door when they knocked."

And they didn't do anything?

"No. They did nothing. They went away."

And nobody ever said anything to you later?

"I am only a poor man, a poor farmer. They did not bother with me."

The meetings in the hamlets usually lasted for several hours. There were speeches by the VC and NLF leaders, almost invariably replete with lavish praise for the people's efforts and sacrifices, claims that their problems were understood and their hardships sympathized with and would later lead to rewards, and that if they had any specific complaints to make, even if such complaints were against the VC, these would be listened to and dealt with at the end of the meeting.

There were long exhortations to work harder for victory, and constant reminders of the necessity to remain vigilant and to do everything to protect their hamlets and their homes if the ARVN and, when the United States entered in force, the Americans attacked; if such an attack came, the people were constantly told, it would mean destruction for their village, rape of their women and death for them—and at some meetings people who said they were from villages far away that had been destroyed by the Americans would spin lurid and gruesome tales of what had happened when the American planes dropped napalm or high explosive bombs, when the ARVN or Korean or American troops had come to their hamlets.

There would be singing, often old traditional folk songs with new words written to the melodies. The words would be recited and the villagers encouraged to join in the singing of these new lyrics. The new lyrics, of course, were fairly blatant damnations of Saigon and the Americans and lavish with praise of the VC and "Uncle Ho."

There were playlets, enacted by small troupes brought along for the purpose or by VC sympathizers from the village who had rehearsed in secret for performances in all the sub-hamlets.

The plays were generally melodramatic parables. There were villains to hiss—Saigon officials and Americans. There was a heroine, a young Vietnamese girl caught, for some reason, in the terrible grasp of the villains and perhaps about to suffer a fate worse than death. And there was the hero, a Vietnamese peasant young man or a young VC soldier who at the last possible moment puts the villains to rout and rescues the heroine. For the viewers, who had rarely been regaled with such entertainment before, it was fascinating and not a little persuasive.

Finally there were questions. The VC leaders listen patiently to all queries and complaints, no matter how minor, petty or self-serving, including denunciations of VC activities in the hamlet. Usually in mild and logical tones, they would attempt to explain why the VC had been doing some of the things to which the people objected. And they would attempt to deal on the spot with any frictions between villagers, not putting off or turning aside but adjudicating such disputes in a firm and fair manner. Everything the people said was treated as though it were of the most momentous nature.

When the meetings finally broke up, the visiting VC and NLF officials departed, leaving behind them a measure of good will, even among those who did not support them. They had entertained the people and had listened to them, and, of course, had propagandized them. The contrast with Saigon's actions when it had been in command—or, rather, its lack of such actions—was not lost on most of the peasants.

What the VC were after, of course, was the unflinching support of the population of Son My (as similar activities were directed at gaining the support of any village in which they were conducted).

But still the VC were Vietnamese, and those VC in any kind of positions of political control in Son My were natives of the village and natives usually of the sub-hamlets where they spent most of their time. They thus knew well enough that, initially at least, there was little chance of winning the unqualified and enthusiastic support of most of the peasants. It was just not the way of these people. Too many things could happen, too many changes in control might occur for the peasants to totally back one side or another. For the peasants, it was best to remain as neutral as possible, giving only that support and cooperation necessary to keep trouble with the VC as far away as possible, to cause as little alteration and deviation from the norm of their daily lives as possible.

So the VC had to be satisfied in Son My, as in any village in an area that was likely to be contested, with whatever cooperation they could get. What they would not brook was outright opposition, and this the people knew full well.

VC officials were often quite blunt when they talked to the people about cooperation and opposition.

If the hamlets and the village cooperated, then they would be supported by the VC and protected by the VC as best they could be protected. If, however, the hamlets refused to cooperate and actively opposed what the VC were trying to do, then there would be great trouble. And much of that trouble would come not just from the VC, though the VC would not hesitate to use their own methods to exact retribution. The troubles would come, as well, from the ARVN, the Koreans and from the Americans with all their massive arms often used indiscriminately. The village would be known as a VC village. This would make it a target for the ARVN and the Americans. If the people cooperated, the VC would not do anything to make the village an immediate target, however. If there was opposition, then the VC could bring the Americans down on the village quickly. One technique that they sometimes used to force the destruction of a recalcitrant hamlet—though they did not use it in the case of most of the hamlets or sub-hamlets of Son My—was to fire on an American patrol from within the settlement. Such fire almost invariably led to an American attack and the settlement's annihilation within a matter of days or weeks.

Cooperation with the VC, however, would not mean just protection by the VC. It would mean, as well, it was frequently emphasized, that most of the people would be left alone most of the time to live as they had always lived. If they cooperated, their lives would not be basically tampered with by their VC overlords.

For the VC, of course, there was considerable advantage in gaining such cooperation, no matter how. The village would provide shelter and manpower. And if it were a prosperous village such as Son My, the taxes assessed in rice could be used to feed large numbers of VC and later NVA in the field.

So for most of the people of Son My, trading the government for the VC meant little change in their existence. As resident after resident told me again and again, when the government was in control, taxes were collected, lectures were given, the young men were taken for the army, but most of the people were left to themselves. When the VC were in control, taxes were collected, lectures were given, young men were taken for the army, but most of the people were left to themselves most of the time. They could farm or fish as they had always done. They could go to market in government-held territory with few restrictions and return home, as long as the traveling was done in daylight— but even in peacetime, the Vietnamese in the countryside is not usually abroad at night. The VC were present but not obtrusive.

The VC's promise of protection from harm in exchange for cooperation proved illusory, as it was bound to. For this was contested territory, not hidden in the jungle but out in the open on the coastline. The arrival of the VC meant that the war had finally come to Son My; the government was not ready to cede control to the VC without some kind of struggle.

A month after the VC arrived, the sub-hamlet of My Khe discovered what it meant to become a battleground.

About two o'clock one morning, three platoons—a little over a hundred men—of ARVN descended on My Khe and the occupying VC force, then a minor holding garrison with most of the men out in the field elsewhere. For about ten minutes before the ARVN fought its way into the sub-hamlet, heavy artillery bombarded My Khe and some of the houses were smashed, a few people killed. Then for about three hours, the ARVN and the VC fought inside and around My Khe with grenades and small arms. Outnumbered, the smaller VC force withdrew about five in the morning, moving back across the Cho Mai River into the Batangan Peninsula, the major VC stronghold in eastern Quang Ngai Province. (Even today, Batangan is considered a VC stronghold. In the last two years, American troops have conducted numerous search-and-destroy missions there, but they admit that it is still under VC domination.)

For the moment the ARVN seemed the victor. It had won a battle from the VC and had re-occupied a strategic point. My Khe was a natural landing spot for supplies coming by water from the north.

But the Arvn had barely time to enjoy its triumph. Within a day, a larger force of VC fell on the ARVN at My Khe and routed the government forces. The VC was back in control.

"After the battles," the former hamlet chief, Le Quang Hai, says, "many people left the area. I left with them. They felt it was no longer safe, that no one could protect them, not the ARVN and not the VC. They hate the fighting, so they left. They hate the death, so they left the area and went away."

Where to?

"Where? To the camps, in Quang Ngai, anywhere."

After its initial foray at My Khe, the ARVN made no major

effort to retake control of Son My village. But ARVN patrols frequently passed through parts of the village, and when they did short skirmishes would erupt. "Every time the ARVN came in," says Nguyen Van Danh, the deputy sub-hamlet chief of My Hoi in Co Luy hamlet, "two or three of our people were killed. Our sub-hamlet did not have good security. It was not safe. So most of the people left the area for years. Some of them stayed in nearby, safer places in the village. Both in our hamlet and in other hamlets. Some went to live with relatives and friends in Xom Lang, in An Thoi and in Don Rang. Sometimes they returned to My Hoi in the daytime to farm their land. At dark they left for safety. Only the poorest people, who had no place to go, stayed in the hamlet."

With each skirmish between ARVN and VC, the sub-hamlets of Son My emptied of their people. But, as Danh notes, many did not go far, merely to one of the nearby hamlets considered a little safer.

In those safer hamlets and sub-hamlets, few of the residents left after the initial exodus at the time of the VC's arrival in 1964. Most hoped that somehow the war would not come near them, and they could not bear to give up their land, to give up their homes, to give up all they knew for an uncertain existence in a refugee camp miles away.

Those who lived in Xom Lang felt themselves particularly fortunate. And they began to believe that the village was truly Thuan Yen, the place where trouble does not come.

Across the road to the south was Elephant Hill which looked down over Xom Lang. Soon after the VC arrived, the South Vietnamese Regional Force constructed an outpost on top of Elephant Hill. There were always soldiers there.

There are some who conjecture that the Ruff-Puffs and the VC struck some kind of bargain. You leave me alone and I'll leave you alone; you stay out of my way and I'll stay out of your way; let's not have trouble right here where some of us are likely to get killed for no reason.

The people of Xom Lang, whatever the truth, felt themselves protected by both the VC and the government against depredations by the other. The few VC who lived in Xom Lang remained hidden during the day, emerging only at night. Higher VC and NLF officials came to Xom Lang only occasionally. The RF's sometimes fired a shot or two into the hamlet but most of the time, like some great bird more fearsome in aspect than in fact, they sat in their outpost on the hill and served as a kind of passive protection.

Even the arrival of massive forces of Americans in Vietnam and their commitment to combat made little difference in this part of Quang Ngai. American planes and choppers would sometimes appear overhead. A number of Son My's sub-hamlets felt the impact of American bombs, and the aftermath of craters, destroyed houses, a few maimed children and some dead. In 1967, the Americans attacked My Khe with napalm and destroyed several buildings, including the Bao Lan Buddhist pagoda.

But in western Quang Ngai, toward the mountains, the commitment to combat by the Americans did bring change. The first major U.S. assault in Vietnam took part in the mountainous area of Quang Ngai. It was called Operation Starlight. It was conducted by the Marines against elements of the 48th VC Local Force Battalion, the same one that operated out of My Khe, and when it was over the Marines claimed they had killed seven hundred of the enemy, leading General William Westmoreland, the American commander in Vietnam, to assert that his Marines "could meet and defeat any force they encounter."

Still the presence of American ground troops was not immediately felt on the coast. This part of Vietnam was theoretically under the military jurisdiction of the ARVN. Before American forces could operate within its confines they were supposed to seek permission and approval from the commander of the ARVN second division and from the ARVN provincial military leaders. In many cases, these commanders were jealous of the fact that the Americans had taken over so much of the country as their own exclusive theatre of operations and relegated the ARVN to a minor role. So they often resisted when American military officers asked for such leave to operate in ARVN territory.

What happened, of course, was that eventually the Americans stopped asking for permission and began operating on their own where they thought they would find VC. They would declare the area a free-fire zone and then move in without informing the ARVN of their plans.

American soldiers began to appear in the area of eastern Quang Ngai near Son My. On a couple of occasions they engaged VC in minor skirmishes in the neighborhood of the hamlets near the beach. But the farther west the Americans moved, the closer they came to ARVN-controlled territory and the RF outpost on Elephant Hill, the less trouble they had.

On three separate occasions in late 1967 and early 1968, American patrols appeared in Xom Lang. Says Nguyen To, a sixty-four year old native of the sub-hamlet, "Three times the GI's operate in my hamlet. They stayed from the morning to six or five in the afternoon every time. They come in, they talked with the people, especially the children who swarmed around them and would say, 'Okay! okay! okay! . . . hello! hello! hello!' And the GI's gave them canned fruits and candy. And the people give the GI's rice and asked the GI's into their houses. At that time the GI's were very friendly. And the people, too, were friendly to them."

Were there shots fired at the GI's from Xom Lang?
"No. No shots."

Were there booby traps or land mines planted around Xom Lang?

"I do not know. But no GI was hurt when they came to our hamlet. Everything was very friendly."

Late in January of 1968, new VC cadres began gathering in My Khe and in other spots in the village where they could mobilize. The Tet offensive was at hand. Some of the people in the hamlets were drafted to serve as weapons and supply carriers, and then the VC moved in toward the provincial capital of Quang Ngai.

For days thereafter the villagers at home heard the sound of rockets and shells and guns reverberating in the distance to the west. Wounded were brought back, hurriedly treated and sent north. Those who had been drafted to carry for the VC brought back stories of ferocious battles in Quang Ngai, of VC successes and then of American counter-attacks with awesome weapons and firepower. Gradually the VC were dislodged from the points they had captured. But still the fighting went on for several weeks.

And then it was over. Many of the VC who had gathered for the offensive and had survived the battles went back to Batangan and wherever else they had come from. Son My settled again into its own routine.

During the day of March 15, some scattered firing was heard in the direction of the coast. Few thought anything about it, for the sound of gunfire had by then become common, part of the known world. In the evening, the story made the rounds that an American patrol had been moving in the neighborhood of My Khe, had been fired upon and had taken a few casualties.

Nobody thought much about the stories. They were just another episode in the war.

And down in My Hoi, in Co Luy hamlet, there was a little celebration that March 15th evening. Some old residents, about a hundred of them, had come home from the refugee camps in Quang Ngai where they had been living for three or four years.

"The government," Nguyen Van Danh, the deputy sub-hamlet chief, says, "came to the camps and told us they had pacified My Hoi. It was safe, they said, and we should go back home. So that afternoon, I arrived home and went back to my old house. I slept there that night."

In Xom Lang and the adjoining sub-hamlet of Binh Dong, the people went to bed with the same confidence that night, as they had for many nights. They were sure that no trouble would come to them. They had not had any trouble for some time. They seemed to get along with the VC without much friction, and the Americans had been friendly when they had come to Xom Lang. There was the RF outpost across the road which seemed to ignore them as they ignored it, except that it seemed a kind of guarantee that everyone would continue to leave them alone. And there had been no leaflets dropped, no helicopter loudspeakers appearing overhead warning the people to leave the area. There was no indication that an attack would come.

So the people of Xom Lang and Binh Dong and of My Hoi went to sleep with the thoughts of work in the fields where the rice was high, almost ready for the first harvest of the year, or a trip to the market the next day, Saturday, March 16.

But there would be no work and few would go to the market. And before noon, their homes and crops and livestock would be destroyed and more than five hundred of them would be dead.

PART TWO

Charley Company

HATE and Fear. Fear and Hate.

These are the emotions that grip most American soldiers during their year in the Vietnamese war zone. Like Siamese twins joined at the heart, they are inextricably linked, one growing from the other, one feeding on the other, but two sides of the same thing. The hate and the fear are in their whole manner when they look at a Vietnamese, when they talk to a Vietnamese. It hangs like a threatening shadow over them when they prepare for a patrol, when they approach a hamlet.

They do not think about the hate and the fear; it is there, all around them, always present. And all around them, too, are the reasons they find for their hate and their fear.

These are nineteen, twenty and twenty-one year old American kids. Most of them have been drafted or have enlisted a moment before the draft reached for them; and this automatically classifies them as apart and, in many of their minds (and the minds of many people back home), as somehow less desirable, less capable, less deserving than the majority of the young men of their generation who have escaped the draft and the army because they are in school or because they have the right connections in their home towns. These young men do not have the educational deferments or the right connections and so their numbers were called and now they are in Vietnam. For many this is the first time they have ever been away from home.

And now they have been shipped to a strange country where the people and the customs are totally alien, unlike anything they had seen before or ever expected to see. They have been given guns and put into a war unlike any war that the United States has ever fought before. They have been told that they will not be in this strange country, in this terrifying war as long as the war lasts, but only a year, twelve months, and if they survive that year they will return home.

Then they have been sent out to fight. But not for territory and not for position and not on battlelines, for no visible gains. They cover the same ground over and over again, conquering and destroying during the day only to discover, when they return again, that the enemy has returned as strong and as much in control as he was before their previous visit.

And this enemy is visibly invisible. He is all around them and yet not around them; he can be anyone they see or no one. And the enemy is not just the people; the enemy is the very ground they walk over, like quicksand that seems as they approach only an innocent patch of bare ground. The land is unfamiliar to them and thus frightening while it is home to the enemy. The enemy can be that field ahead, littered perhaps with land mines; the enemy can be that grove of trees, booby-trapped to kill or maim anything and anyone coming within its range; the enemy can be that turn in the dim road ahead, where an ambush may be waiting.

The enemy can be the little kid, five or six years old, in the next hamlet who comes out smiling, yelling, "Okay! Okay! Hello! Hello! Chao! Chao!" and then pulls his hand out from behind his back and lobs a grenade. The enemy can be that bent old lady struggling across another field carrying a watermelon in her arms, a watermelon that is a booby trap she will plant somewhere for an unsuspecting GI to pick up and blow himself to hell.

If you are an American soldier, young and inexperienced, you will be afraid and filled with hatred. And everyone will soon become your enemy, the object of that fear and hate, for if you trust no one—for you soon feel that none can be trusted—and hate everyone, maybe you will survive.

It is one thing to fight in the mountains against the North Vietnamese. They dress in green uniforms; they are identifiable; they are almost as unfamiliar with the ground as you are. A number of anguished letters have been found on the bodies of North Vietnamese officers complaining to their VC counterparts about their unfamiliarity with the territory and pleading both for experienced guides and for better marked mine fields and booby traps, for NVA soldiers, according to one letter I saw, had been stumbling into VC mine fields and booby traps and getting killed.

It is another thing to fight in the east, in VC country. For the uniform of the VC is the dress of the peasant, the black tunics and black pants, the familiar black pajamas. Is everyone wearing black pajamas VC? Not likely, since everyone wears black pajamas. How, you think, can a six year old be the enemy? How can a seventy year old grandmother, frail and feeble, be the enemy?

But they can be and so you have to hate six-year-olds and seventy-year-olds, you have to hate children and old people, you have to hate and fear all Vietnamese.

You don't, of course, know any Vietnamese. You came to Vietnam straight from the United States, entering the country usually through the huge American base at Cam Ranh Bay. From Cam Ranh Bay you went to your unit's base, to Chu Lai if you are assigned to the Americal Division and the I Corps area. Chu Lai is just a little bit of America moved across the sea, and you could be back home at a base camp somewhere in the states. There are few Vietnamese around.

From Chu Lai your unit moves on to a fire base, an LZ, or a landing zone (since you are supplied by helicopters), as they are often called. There are only other Americans there. And when you began to patrol the hostile countryside which rings the LZ, you are again with Americans.

What Vietnamese do you see to get to know? There is the occasional interpreter assigned to your company so that someone can talk with the people in the "villes," as you come to call the hamlets. But he is aloof, attached to the officers not to you, and there are times as you watch him when you wonder why the hell he's got such a cushy job when you're out fighting for his country.

There is, of course, the old couple, the mamma-san and the pappa-san, who come to clean your hootch and to do odd, menial chores around the base or at the LZ. They are bent and servile, rarely saying anything, obsequious in their seeming desire to please, in their bending to your every wish. You have no idea what they're thinking, and you couldn't really care less. They are more like pet dogs, to be petted sometimes and to be booted at others, but to be ignored most of the time.

Vietnamese merchants operate near the base. They, you are certain, must be taking advantage of you and every American, and sneering at you while they do. Like the old guy outside Chu Lai who makes NVA and VC battleflags to sell to American soldiers as war souvenirs. He makes them, rips them, grinds them in the mud, pours chicken blood over them to make them look as though they were taken straight off the body of a dead VC or NVA. And then he charges high prices for them, perhaps a thousand piastres for one of those flags. You tell your friends and you tell visitors from the states, pointing him out, that he's just another one of those damn war profiteers, leeching off Americans.

If you get rest-and-recreation leave ("R-and-R") and decide not to go to Taiwan or Tokyo or Hong Kong or Honolulu or Bangkok, but to Saigon instead, what kind of Vietnamese do you see there? That is, if you even bother to leave the R-and-R center near Ton Son Nhut air base and the company of other Americans.

You see the black marketeer, guys who are selling stuff straight from the PX, stuff you know is stolen. You see the money changers, guys who are willing to change your "green" —real dollars—or M.P.C.'s—military procurement certificates—for piastres. They may offer you three hundred or three hundred fifty P's to the dollar when the legal rate you can change your money at through the army or the banks is a hundred eighteen to the dollar. So you go with them into some dingy, urine-smelling back alley with rats as big as dogs scrounging in the dirt and little kids with only shirts and no pants standing by watching you with big eyes. Maybe they will change your money as they said, but the chances are better than even that they'll pull a shell game on you right while your watching, and you'll never catch on that they've short-changed you until an hour later when you start to count the money. Or maybe, back there in that alley, a bunch of them will jump you, take everything you've got and leave you bruised and bleeding in the dirt. And how the hell can you complain? You've been breaking the law yourself by dealing with the black market. And even if you do complain, go to the M.P.'s and the Quan's (the Quan Canh's, the Vietnamese military police), what good is it going to do you? You can't tell one Vietnamese from another so how would you know even if they picked up the right guys.

And there are the kids, tiny, hardly up to your chest, moving in packs down Tu Do and Le Loi and the rest of the streets in the center of Saigon. The first time you see them you don't think much, until they suddenly surround you, hit and are gone, and it takes you a minute to realize that they've emptied your pockets and even taken the watch right off your wrist. The next time you see a bunch of kids, they don't look so appealing and you're ready with a closed fist if they come near you. Your face shows how you feel.

B girls, too, ply their trade at all the bars and gyp joints that line Tu Do from the Caravalle Hotel right down to the Saigon River. Most of the time they'll have you sitting at the bar with them all night, drinking and paying for their drinks. When it's time to score, suddenly a boy friend shows up on a motorbike and she's gone. You're left on the sidewalk with an empty wallet and a put-down face. If you try to stop her from going off, object at all, then a bunch of Vietnamese, little guys but tough, are likely to climb all over you and the M.P.'s and the Quan's are likely to haul you in, and that's the end of your leave.

Even if you do score, what happens? You wind up with a dose of clap or syph, and probably rolled in the process.

These are the only Vietnamese in Saigon, or in any of the cities, that you have anything to do with. You never get to know them, know what they're thinking and what they want, and you probably don't want to get to know any of these people. And the higher-class Vietnamese, those girls in their immaculate white au dais whom you occasionally glimpse riding by in a pedi-cab, or even, early in the evening, riding with their black-gloved hands on the handlebars of their own motorbikes or on the backs of their equally immaculate and haughty boy friends' motorbikes, they don't want anything to do with you. They turn their backs if you try to approach them and make some comment in Vietnamese whose meaning you can guess.

Here you are, fighting in their country, risking your life everytime you go out on patrol and they're out to take you for everything you've got or they think you're something low and they don't want anything to do with you. And they're sitting around Saigon, far away from the war. They don't seem to be risking a damn thing, certainly not their lives. You look at those guys roaring around Saigon on their motorbikes, those guys pulling the B girls away from you, those guys changing money and peddling stuff from the PX and you have some pretty bitter thoughts about why they're not in the ARVN. Why the hell should you have to fight while they sit around and make a killing?

So you go back to your unit, back to the fire base, back to patrolling the hostile countryside. And there are the Vietnamese you see when you go on patrol. That's where you really learn to fear and hate.

You walk down a road, any road, between the rice paddies. There are Vietnamese in every paddy, in their black pajamas and conical hats, bent over, working, looking like some picture postcard you bought back at base and sent home. None of them looks up when you pass. They act as though you aren't even there. Then, all of a sudden, a mortar shell lands right in the middle of the patrol and a couple of guys you've been buddies with since you got in country are dead and a couple of others are screaming in agony, maybe with a leg or an arm blown off or their guts hanging out. You, and everyone else, drop to the side of the road, taking cover, scanning everywhere rapidly to find out where that damn mortar came from. But all those Vietnamese peasants are still working in the paddies just like they were before, as though nothing at all had happened. Did one of them lob the mortar? If so, which one? Should you kill all of them, none of them? Should you take them all in? What should you do?

You go into a ville and everybody gathers in the square, smiling, nodding, saying "Okay" and "Hello" and "Chao" and "No VC, no VC." It's like your old man told you it was when they liberated some town back in France or Italy in his war. You pass out your rations and some candy and cigarettes, and then some old lady or some little kid or somebody hidden in one of those hootches tosses a grenade at a bunch of you. Then you know they're all nothing but VC, so you shoot up a little and the "Zippo Squad" takes out its lighters and turns those hootches into torches.

Or maybe everything is just fine in that ville while you're there. They even share their rice with you (though you notice that there aren't many young girls around, say between fifteen and twenty, and those who are around are pregnant). When you're ready to leave, some of them even walk with you to the end of the ville, smiling, shaking your hand, and then letting you walk right into a mine field or a bunch of booby traps that have been sitting there just waiting for you. They haven't said a word to warn you. And sometimes they'll even direct you straight into that mine field or those booby traps, telling you all the time that it's the safest way out the ville. Maybe—not maybe, you become certain—they've planted those damn mines and booby traps and set you up.

Even if none of that happens, you begin to grow certain it's going to happen everytime you go into a ville, everytime you go anywhere near the Vietnamese.

And you become convinced that they're ungrateful for what you're doing for them, that they don't give a damn whether you live or die, in fact would probably like to see you dead. Say you get a patrol, get on a CAP team protecting a resettlement camp. You pass out your rations and other stuff to these people right after the supply chopper comes in. But if that chopper's late by a couple of days with your supplies and you've run short of food, do you think these people are going to return what you gave them because you need it now? Like hell. They'll sell it back to you, at a price, and a damn high one, but they won't give it back.

Pretty soon you get to hate all these people. You get to fear them, too. They're all out for your ass one way or another, out to take you for everything you've got. You don't know which ones are your enemies and which ones are your friends. So you begin to think that they're all your enemies. And that all of them are something not quite human, some kind of lower order of creature. You give them names to depersonalize them, to categorize them as you've become convinced they ought to be categorized. They become dinks and slopes and slants and gooks, and you begin to say, and believe, "The only good dink is a dead dink." You echo the comments of your buddies that, "One million of them ain't worth one of us. We should blow up all those slant-eyed bastards."

Even the little kids, even the babies. "Shit, they're gonna grow up one of these days and learn how to use a rifle. One of those kids is gonna throw a grenade and kill a good guy. You kill 'em young, they won't get no chance to do that."

You have forgotten, though it is unlikely that you ever knew, why you were sent to Vietnam to fight. You have forgotten, if you ever even thought about it, that Vietnam is the country of the Vietnamese, not the country of Americans.

So you hate and fear the Vietnamese, all Vietnamese, for all these reasons. And you hate them and fear them because you are convinced it is because of them that you are in Vietnam in peril of death or maiming and not at home where you want to be.

I sit on the terrace of the Continental Palace Hotel in Saigon on a warm evening, drinking Saigon beer and talking with a Vietnamese poet who, now that there is no place for poetry in Vietnam, has become an ARVN major. The talk turns to the mine fields and the booby traps in the hamlets and villages of the war zones, of how Americans feel about Vietnamese and how Vietnamese feel about Americans.

"The Americans don't seem to understand," the poet and major says, "that when they come into a hamlet most of the

71

people don't look at them as liberators or protectors. They don't feel that the Americans have come to free them from some terrible overlord, the VC, to free them from some terrible oppression. Perhaps it is because of the stories they have heard from relatives in other hamlets and the propaganda they have heard for so long from the VC. But they see the Americans as foreign invaders who have come to destroy their homes, to rape their women, to kill them. Some of them will take an action to protect themselves and their homes from these invaders. The little boy, the old women, the people who throw grenades at the Americans, they are heroes to many of the people in their hamlets. They have risked their lives to protect their people from these invaders."

But the Americans have been to a lot of these hamlets before without ever doing anything. In fact, most of the time they've been pretty friendly to the people, giving them things.

"That's true. But the people suspect. They say to themselves, and the VC tell them, this time the Americans did nothing, but next time . . . and too often next time the Americans do something, and people in other hamlets hear about it."

So they throw grenades? And they plant mines and booby traps, too, for the same reason? To protect themselves?

"The VC force many of them to do that. But sometimes they are not hard to force, for they do it also with the idea that they are protecting themselves. Tell me, if foreign invaders came to an American village, what would the people do? Would they not do everything they could to fight these invaders? Would they not do it especially if they had been told and believed that their homes were going to be destroyed, their women raped and they themselves killed?"

The men of Company C began to arrive at Schofield Barracks in Hawaii in December of 1966, shipped in from basic training all over the United States, these American kids become soldiers, most of them still teen-agers or just barely out of their teens. Through the first half of 1967 they would keep coming until they numbered about a hundred and fifty.

At basic training, they had learned the rudiments of being soldiers; now they would learn to be a company, putting aside for these years such civilian fancies as individualism. When they had begun to develop as a unit, they would be shipped across the Pacific to a strange country of which many of them, only a few years before, had never even heard.

In Vietnam, they would become Company C, First Battalion, Twentieth Infantry, a rifle company. Together with two other rifle companies training at Schofield Barracks—in Vietnam to be called Company A, Third Battalion, First Infantry, and Company B, Fourth Battalion, Third Infantry—they would be welded into a new brigade, the Eleventh Brigade, and assigned under the command of the Americal Division in the northern I Corps area. The brigade, commanded in its first months in Vietnam by Brigadier General Andy L. Lipscomb, would be named "Task Force Barker," after its executive officer, Lieutenant Colonel Frank A. Barker, already a veteran of one tour in Vietnam.

As the first of these one hundred and fifty men of Company C arrived in Hawaii, they found their commanders waiting for them. In charge of this unit was Captain Ernest L. Medina, just thirty and, except for a couple of veteran Army sergeants, the oldest man in Charley Company.

Born in Springer, New Mexico, in 1936, of Mexican-American parents, Medina's early years were hard ones, a constant struggle. His mother died when he was only two months old and a couple of months later his father shipped him off to live with grandparents in the tiny town of Montrose, Colorado. It was bad enough to be a Mexican-American in a town where Mexican-Americans were at the bottom of the social scale, but to this was added, as it is for many of Mexican background in the west, constant financial worry. All through his early years, Medina worked to supplement the meager funds available to his grand-parents—he delivered papers, worked as a soda jerk and in a local supermarket. And in school, he was just about average, neither failing in anything nor excelling.

But if there was one thing that moved him early in his life, it was a love of his country. He became a patriot, dreamed of becoming a soldier, and in 1956, at the age of twenty, he enlisted in the Army. By the Army's criteria, he was a good soldier, advancing through the enlisted ranks, going on to officer candidate school and, eight years after his enlistment, being commissioned a second lieutenant, having graduated fourth in his class of more than two hundred. Twice he served in Germany where he married an East German refugee. He was considered a good officer, bright and able to command, with the ability to improvise when the situation required it.

In early December of 1966, Medina shipped out for Hawaii. His assignment: take charge of a new company and turn a raw group of young men, mainly draftees, into a company for Vietnam. In the process of doing this he won a nickname from his fellow officers—"Mad Dog" Medina.

Under Medina there were the young lieutenants, themselves new to war and hurriedly trained. In charge of the second platoon was Lieutenant Stephen Brooks, one of the most popular young officers among the men in Charley Company; he would die in action in Vietnam. The leader of the third platoon was another popular young officer, Lieutenant Jeffrey La Cross; his men came to feel that they could depend on his judgment in crisis. And, to run the first platoon Medina was assigned Lieutenant William Laws Calley, Jr.

Born in Miami, Florida, in 1943, Calley was a small, slim man—five foot three inches, a hundred thirty pounds—with reddish-brown hair that had brought him the boyhood nick-name of Rusty. There was an intense look about his eyes which some of his men noticed and commented on, and which was later to perturb some of them.

Calley was an average American boy. Born into a middle-class family, he had few worries during his early years. His father, a Navy veteran, was a successful salesman of heavy construction equipment and had both a comfortable home in Miami and a vacation retreat in Waynesville, North Carolina. Calley and his three sisters lived a relaxed, easy life between the two homes, and Calley, too small to play on school teams but a sports lover nevertheless, was often found on the playing fields. In school, his marks were considered about average; there was nothing distinctive about him, nothing that brings him back particularly to his former teachers, that signals him out from his friends.

After ninth grade at Edison High School in Miami, Calley was sent off to Georgia Military Academy. But the military life did not appeal to him then. "He wanted to come home," a friend recalled. "Finally he did. He seemed to want to forget it. He didn't dig it." So, after two years in military school, Calley returned to Miami and Edison High School for his senior year. Graduated, he went on to Palm Beach Junior College in Lake Worth, Florida, but higher education proved not for him: he flunked out after a year with grades in seven courses of two C's, one D and four F's.

Out of school, Calley drifted. He left home and moved in with a couple of friends, worked for a while as a bellhop at a West Palm Beach hotel, quit and became a restaurant dish-washer. This was hardly the kind of job that he considered worthy of himself and so he looked around for other work. He found it, as a strikebreaker. The Florida East Coast Railway had been hit by a strike and was trying to hire non-union men, often at higher wages than the strikers were asking, in order both to break the strike and keep running. In July of 1963, Calley, then twenty, applied and got a job as a switchman. A few months later he was promoted to conductor on a freight train, the youngest conductor in the system. Less than a year on the job and he was arrested in Fort Lauderdale for allowing his train of forty-seven cars to block traffic for more than a half-hour during the rush hour. The judge, however, acquitted him when Calley explained that the brakes on the train had malfunctioned.

But there were other troubles ahead. His mother developed cancer and lingered in bed, deteriorating until she died in mid-1966. His father's business started to go bad and then the firm he worked for went bankrupt. And Calley's father developed diabetes which steadily worsened, disabling him. He sold the family home in Miami and moved north to North Carolina for a couple of years. Today he and his youngest daughter live in a trailer in Florida.

Calley left Miami at the same time his family did, telling his friends that he was heading for California and then vanishing from their lives completely, leaving no forwarding address and not writing to anyone (his father was later to say, when the investigation of the massacre broke into print, that he had not heard from his son in many months). Buying a new Buick Wildcat with the money he had accumulated working for the railroad—at times he had earned as much as $300 a week—he took the road westward. No one seems quite sure what he did for the next year and a half, though there are stories among his friends that for a time he was a real estate photographer and an insurance appraiser in New Mexico.

But the Army was closing in. While in Miami, Calley had been classified 1-Y, a medical deferment because of ulcers he developed at nineteen. Shortly before leaving Miami he was reclassified 1-A. With a call just about certain, he enlisted in the Army in July of 1966 at Albuquerque. Now the Army seemed to appeal to him and the military saw potential in him which had apparently escaped those who dealt with him as a civilian. He was sent to Officers Candidate School at Fort Benning, Georgia, graduated somewhere in the middle of his class without any particular distinction, and was commissioned a second lieutenant, then sent off to take command of the first platoon of Medina's Charley Company.

Under Medina and his officers—Calley, La Cross and Brooks —were the sergeants who ran the army, for the most part professional army men, dedicated and tough soldiers for whom this was just another way station in a career that would extend twenty or twenty-five or more years to retirement. These were men like Sergeant Harry Hobscheid, an eighteen-year veteran and Medina's own sergeant; Sergeant Charles Cox, a squad leader for Lieutenant Brooks, a charismatic man whose death a short time before the attack on Son My would depress just about everyone in the company; Staff Sergeant David Mitchell, a squad leader in Calley's platoon. A native of St. Francisville, Louisiana, Mitchell was then twenty-seven and had spent seven years in the Army. Born in rural Louisiana, like any black man in the early 1960's in the south, he had gone to segregated schools. But unlike many, he had finished, graduating from high school. Once out, he joined an Army reserve unit and when it was activated he decided to remain in the Army for life. He served tours of duty in Germany, Korea and Hawaii, rose through the ranks to sergeant and "felt at home" in the army. He was a good, tough leader and most of the men under him knew that when he gave an order it was to be obeyed without question.

Then there were the enlisted men who would learn in Hawaii that their lives in combat depended on the actions and reactions of each other, that they had to learn to work as a team if they were to survive.

There were men like Private (now Sergeant) Michael Bernhardt of Franklin Square, Long Island, who quit the University of Miami early in 1967 before finishing his junior year. He wanted to enlist in the Army and to fight in Vietnam. He knew little about the war or about what was happening in Vietnam but, he said, he had "absolute faith" that what his government was doing was right. Besides, he felt that being a soldier was one phase in every man's life and he might as well live through it. As for going to Vietnam, "When the country's involved in a conflict, that's where a soldier is supposed to be."

There were others, too. Charles West of Chicago was a good soldier, rarely gave his superiors any trouble and in Vietnam when Sergeant Cox was killed he became sergeant and squad leader replacing him. There were Vernardo Simpson of Jackson, Mississippi, who became an assistant squad leader under Calley; Private Herbert Carter of Houston, who would be the company's only casualty on the March day in 1968; he would shoot himself in the foot. There was James Bergthold of Niagara Falls, and Charles Gruver of Tulsa, Oklahoma, called Butch. There was Robert Wilson of Bloomington, Indiana, called Bobby, probably the most popular private in the company, always ready with a joke or a quip, filled with the gallows humor of the firebase; in February of 1968, he would step on a land mine and die, at nineteen. There was Paul Meadlo of Terre Haute, Indiana, Bobby Wilson's best friend; the day after the massacre he would step on a land mine and lose his foot and feel that perhaps it was a just retribution; and nearly two years later he would go on television and tell his story of that day. There were John Kinch and Michael Terry of Utah, Lenny Lagunoy and Leon Stevenson, William Doherty of Boston, James Olson, Kenneth Hodges of Dublin, Georgia, Esequiel Torres of Brownsville, Max Hutson of Indiana, Gerald Smith of Chicago, and Charles Hutto of Tallulah, Louisiana. For their part in the events of that March morning, Smith, Hodges, Hutson, and Hutto would be charged by the Army with murder, attempted murder, and rape.

These and more—all told about one hundred and fifty men—were the men whom Ernest Medina and his officers took in those months of 1967 in Hawaii and tried to turn into a tough company of warriors prepared to meet any exigency in Vietnam.

By December it was thought that they were ready. On December 5, 1967, Charley Company moved out on its way to Vietnam, the advance guard of the new Eleventh Brigade. The other companies would follow a few days later. But Medina's company was given the honor of being the first because, its commander later said, it had the highest level of combat preparedness.

The war in Vietnam to which the new Eleventh Brigade, Task Force Barker, moved that December had become almost entirely an American war. The South Vietnamese Army was pushed further and further out of the mainstream of the fighting and more than 500,000 American soldiers, sailors and marines were meeting, when they could find them, a smaller force of Viet Cong guerrillas and regular troops from the North Vietnamese Army. This turn from an internal Vietnamese struggle into a war engaging on one side troops of North Vietnam and Vietnamese guerrillas armed and supplied by North Vietnam, China, the Soviet Union and other Soviet bloc nations; and on the other troops from the United States, Korea, the Philippines, Australia, South Vietnam and others—all, save the American, Korean and South Vietnamese in minor supporting roles and numbers—had been accomplished in only a little over two years.

When John Kennedy was assassinated on November 22, 1963, only twenty-two days after the overthrow of the Diem regime in Saigon, the American role in Vietnam, though growing, was still a limited one. There were then about 14,000 American

soldiers in Vietnam, certainly a vast increase from the 2,000 who
had been in country on that January day in 1961 when Kennedy had taken his oath of office. But their role, nonetheless, was
still a limited one. Theoretically they were in Vietnam to train
Vietnamese to fight their own war in what was still considered a
civil struggle, and though some of these American military
advisers were leading ARVN troops on patrols and engaging in
limited actions, this was supposed to be clandestine, not to be
spoken aloud. By the time of President Kennedy's death, though
growing, the American role was still minor and only about 110
American soldiers had been killed in the fighting.

Against considerable pressure from the military establishment
in the Pentagon and in Saigon, the Kennedy Administration, and
particularly the President himself, seemed determined to keep
Vietnam, as far as American involvement went, a "limited war."
Kennedy would supply the Saigon government with the arms
and matériel it needed to wage the struggle against the Viet
Cong, then its principal enemy since North Vietnamese Army
troops had not then put in an appearance, but to limit the
involvement of Americans to the peripheral sphere of advisers.
The guiding motif of the Kennedy vision of the Vietnamese
struggle was perhaps best expressed by the President during a
television interview in September, 1963. According to Arthur
Schlesinger, Jr., the President threw away a mild statement on
Vietnam prepared for him by his staff and spoke instead his
own feelings: "In the first analysis, it is their war. They are the
ones who have to win it or lose it. We can help them, we can
give them equipment, we can send our men out there as advisers,
but they have to win it, the people of Vietnam."

Despite his own inclinations, however, Kennedy, under constant pressure from the military, had begun the process of escalation which would be carried forward and enlarged grossly by
his successor. But Kennedy, disenchanted with the military after

the fiasco of the Bay of Pigs invasion of Cuba, seemed always to look at what the military was saying with a jaundiced gaze. If he sent some troops to Vietnam at the military's behest, he sent nowhere near what they were constantly requesting and while the military viewed Vietnam, as had Dwight Eisenhower's Secretary of State John Foster Dulles, as a crucial battleground to halt and roll back communism in Asia and particularly Communist China, Kennedy continued to view it innately as an internal conflict which should be isolated and limited as far as possible.

Lyndon Johnson, however, did not have the same dyspeptic view of the military as did Kennedy. Though Vice President at the time of the Bay of Pigs, he had not been personally stung by bad advice from the military as Kennedy had, and so he seemed more willing to rely on the judgment of the military chiefs at the Pentagon and of the generals and intelligence officers in Saigon. And their view of the struggle in Vietnam was abetted by Secretary of State Dean Rusk with his apocalyptic vision of the machinations of "international communism," and to a lesser extent by the Secretary of Defense Robert McNamara, who seemed as the years passed an increasingly reluctant hawk. Further, Johnson himself inclined to the view that the struggle in Vietnam was a struggle against communism, and this belief had been enchanced when as Vice President he had toured that country and spoken with Diem.

Thus on taking office in November 1963, Johnson, gazing at the war from the situation room of the White House and privy now to all the intelligence reports which Kennedy had tended to discount, saw only confirmation of the biases of his generals and of himself. Indeed, only two days after Kennedy's assassination, Johnson and McNamara gave a secret unconditional pledge of military support to the government of South Vietnam—though it is doubtful if either at that moment understood what that pledge would ultimately entail.

In the first six months of his administration, the pressures on Johnson to escalate the war by major strides were mounting from both the military and the Central Intelligence Agency. But at that point, the president was more than a little reluctant to immediately follow such advice, though he was prepared to take other steps to bolster Saigon's will and desire to continue the fight.

In Vietnam, however, during the first months of the Johnson administration, the popular movement was in the opposite direction—toward compromise and negotiations with the National Liberation Front leading to neutrality when peace came. To counter this, Johnson sent a New Year's message to General Duong Van (Big) Minh, leader of the junta which had overthrown Diem, asserting that "neutralization of South Vietnam would be only another name for a Communist take-over."

And, with what many are convinced was covert American assistance, a plot to replace Minh with a government more to the liking of Washington began to gather force. At the end of January, in a lightning coup, Minh was out, replaced by General Nguyen Khanh. He promised an all-out fight against the Viet Cong and even began to shout for *bac tien*, or "to the North." Washington immediately gave the new Khanh regime its promise of total support.

But Khanh, despite all his rhetoric, was totally ineffectual in stemming the VC advance. The VC was on the offensive; it decimated the ARVN wherever it met that army; it increasingly enhanced its control over the countryside to the extent that even the Americans were forced to admit in April of 1964 that the VC controlled more than 40 per cent of the Vietnamese villages and another 25 per cent were neutral. And the Saigon government was on the verge of collapse; with just a little more effort, the war would be over, the VC victors.

The Johnson administration took its first steps to escalation.

The American troop strength was increased by 30 per cent, to 21,000 men and for the first time the military admitted that American soldiers had permission to fire on the enemy if fired upon (of course, this had been the practice for some time).

But even if Johnson had desired at that time to take further action, events on the American domestic scene limited him. Vietnam had increasingly become an issue in presidential politics. Barry Goldwater, the Republican candidate, was that summer and fall of 1964 calling for a major expansion of the war into the North, a drive to win. And Richard Nixon, campaigning for Goldwater and at the same time enhancing his own status with Republicans for the future, was declaring that "the goal of the South Vietnamese Army must be a free North Vietnam and . . . the war must be carried north to achieve that goal."

Johnson, on the other hand, was presenting himself to the American voters as the peace candidate, deriding Nixon and Goldwater for their hawkish statements and asserting that he wanted "no wider war."

If Johnson could, then, win support of peace groups by contrasting his stand with that of the Republicans, he was also given the opportunity to at least partially counter the thrust of those who wanted to carry the war north and fight on to victory. The opportunity came early in August in what was surely the crucial event in the history of the American involvement in Vietnam, and Johnson's response took the edge off the Goldwater cries that the United States was standing by and watching Vietnam go down the drain and with that country, echoing the domino obsession of Dulles a decade before, all of Southeast Asia.

This was the episode in the Tonkin Gulf. On the night of August 2, North Vietnamese torpedo boats attacked the U.S. destroyer Maddox as it cruised in international waters in the Gulf of Tonkin off the North Vietnamese island of Hon Me. In the official Washington version, this was an unprovoked attack; in Hanoi's version, it was a reprisal for American bombardment of Hon Me and other nearby North Vietnamese islands.

Two days later came the major crisis, supposedly another attack by North Vietnamese torpedo boats—but there is considerable doubt whether such an attack ever even occurred. According to the Pentagon at the time, the Maddox was joined that night by another U.S. destroyer, the Turner Joy, and both were cruising some sixty-five miles off the North Vietnamese coast, when a squadron of torpedo boats launched the new "unprovoked attack." No damage was done to the destroyers and no casualties were suffered; the Americans claimed they drove the attackers off and destroyed two of them in the process.

There is considerable doubt, in the light of evidence gathered since, that any attack occurred at all. And there is also considerable evidence that the Maddox had been provoking the North Vietnamese for a considerable time. It and other American ships had been supporting South Vietnamese commando raids on the North Vietnamese mainland and in the Gulf of Tonkin. Further, the Maddox was equipped with sophisticated electronic gear, was in all essentials an ELINT, or an electronics intelligence ship. Between August 1 and August 4, it had on several occasions simulated attacks on North Vietnam, driving in toward the shore with its gun control radar turned on as though it were about to shoot at targets, and in so doing it had violated the twelve-mile limits which North Vietnam claimed as its territory. Its object, of course, was to assess the North Vietnamese defenses. Finally, on the night of August 4—a pitch black night with limited vision—the only reported sighting was of a torpedo wake by the inexperienced crew of the Turner Joy.

Nevertheless, after much debate within the administration's highest circles, the reports from the Turner Joy were accepted as the truth. President Johnson and his administration were not prepared to accept such "unprovoked attacks" without a major response. Taking to television on the night of August 4, the President announced that "air action is now in execution against gunboats and certain supporting facilities in North Vietnam which have been used in these hostile operations."

And the President then went to Congress for backing. It responded with the unlimited Tonkin Gulf Resolution which was to be used as the key to all the later events in Vietnam. The resolution asserted that "all measures will be taken to repulse aggression and prevent further aggression." Johnson had a blank check from Congress to do as he would in Vietnam in the years to follow.

The first escalation of the war, and the first step toward major American entrapment in it had been taken.

The pressures on the President to do more mounted, but even then he still resisted. The presidential campaign and the magnitude of his victory led Johnson to keep a blanket over any administration plans to step up the war. Those would await further developments after the inauguration in January.

Only two weeks later, the next major leap in widening the war was taken. On February 5, 1965, the Viet Cong attacked with mortars, rockets, machine guns and small arms the American base at Pleiku. Nine American soldiers were killed and 140 were wounded. In what the Administration called a reprisal for this raid and a "test of will," where not to respond would have been to prove a paper tiger, a wave of American planes conducted a major air strike at North Vietnam. The war, American involvement in it, had escalated again.

But domestic events in South Vietnam led to the next major step. Government instability was at its height, and with each new change, the government in power seemed more ineffectual and incompetent than the one it had succeeded. January and

February 1965 were marked by a series of coups and attempted coups. Finally, in late February, the United States found the strong man it had been seeking. A military dictatorship under Air Marshall Nguyen Cao Ky, who had led air strikes to the north and had increasingly called for expanding the war to North Vietnam, took command. With the advent of Ky came tougher talk and, in Saigon, all talk in government circles of a negotiated peace and an end to the war came to an end. Ky's Premier Phan Huy Quat declared on March 1 that the war was "obviously a case of self-defense." And, he said, South Vietnam would fight on until the "communists end the war they have provoked and stop their infiltration."

The finger had been pointed now by Vietnamese, as well as Washington, at North Vietnam as the villain behind the Viet Cong. The call for a holy war against communist aggression had been sounded. Johnson, with the Tonkin Gulf Resolution in his holster to give him total authority to do as he would, responded. On March 2, 1965, American bombers attacked North Vietnam again. But this time no excuse of "retaliation" was given. There had been no particular event to spark this raid. It was carrying the war to the north, to the "aggressor," and the next step in escalation had been taken.

Now American escalation on the ground moved apace with the war in the air. Within days of the air strikes over North Vietnam, the first wave of United States Marines landed in Vietnam. By the end of June there were 53,500 American troops "in country" as the Americans came to say. And the fiction that they were merely advisers, that they would shoot only when shot at, was dropped. The marines, and the army troops as they followed, began to mount patrols on their own; began to seek out the enemy and not to wait for him to strike.

As American involvement deepened, so too did that of Hanoi. The North Vietnamese began to take countersteps, sending a growing stream of their own troops south. From a trickle, averaging less than 600 NVA soldiers a month in 1963 and 1,000 a month in 1964, the flow of NVA troops south increased to 4,500 a month in 1965 and 5,000 a month in 1966.

Such counter-escalation by North Vietnam was more than matched by Washington. By mid-1966, the number of American troops in South Vietnam had soared to 267,000 and American bombers had begun plastering the oil depots around Hanoi and Haiphong.

Neither American troops nor planes seemed capable of either turning back the NVA in its flow south or of beating the VC and the NVA on their home ground, in the villages and hamlets of the South Vietnamese countryside. A further American escalation was mounted. Declaring that Hanoi had turned "jungle trails into all-weather roads" to ship men and supplies south, President Johnson announced even further American buildups. By the end of 1966, there were 375,000 American troops in Vietnam; a year later, the number was up to 525,000. These American troops combined with about 50,000 Koreans, Philippine soldiers and other allies, and about 600,000 to a million ARVN—though the ARVN was taking more and more of a subsidiary role as the war became more and more Americanized, costing the United States heavy casualities and more than $30-billion a year—faced about 270,000 VC regulars and guerrillas and another 30,000 North Vietnamese Army troops. From a small internal struggle in the early 1960's through Kennedy's minor escalations that broadened but still limited the war, Vietnam had now become a major battleground.

This, then, was where Vietnam had come when Task Force Barker landed on its shores in early December of 1967.

The Task Force was attached to the Americal Division in the I Corps area—the northern five provinces of Vietnam—perhaps the center of the most intensive American efforts. It was the bastion of strong and long-lived VC operations, where the elusive VC 48th Local Force Battalion held sway, and aside from the major cities of Hue, Da Nang and Quang Ngai and a few others, the rural countryside was considered "Indian Country," almost totally under VC control.

Throughout I Corps, the American emphasis was on continuous search-and-destroy missions, with much of the rural area considered free-fire zones. At first the operations in the area had been centered in what was called Task Force Oregon. But in September of 1967, Task Force Oregon was disbanded and the I Corps was turned over to the newly re-organized Americal Division.* With more than 40,000 men under its banner, the division was the largest of the four operating in I Corps, and of any in Vietnam. I Corps had more American troops than any other area. In January of 1968, in another major buildup in the area, and additional 30,000 American soldiers were sent in, bringing U.S. strength in I Corps to 170,000 men, or a third of all American forces in Vietnam. This, said General Westmoreland, is "a real war zone."

The Eleventh Brigade, with Medina's Charley Company, was dispatched almost as soon as it arrived in Vietnam to a base at Duc Pho in the southern part of Quang Ngai Province, the southern sector of I Corps. Just before Christmas, Charley Company moved out for its first taste of combat, setting up operations at a nearby fire base called Gilligan's Island. From there it would mount patrols and missions into the surrounding hostile countryside.

Christmas came and it could not be ignored. Medina and Sergeant Hobscheid decided to see if they could round up an old

* The Americal was named for a division set up hastily by General Douglas MacArthur in the South Pacific during the early stages of World War II—hence its shoulder patch showing the "Southern Cross." It was the Army's unit that would operate with or slightly behind the Marines in amphibious assaults on the Japanese-held islands.

88

fashioned Christmas dinner, to bring some taste of America to these men so far from home. Hobscheid managed to "liberate" from somewhere tables, chairs and the equipment for a mess hall. The food came and the men, in green fatigues with weapons at hand and ready for battle despite the temporary Christmas cease-fire declared by all sides, dined and celebrated at Gilligan's Island that December 25, 1968, the birth of the Prince of Peace.

And then the war arrived. Patrols began to move out daily. Still there was almost no action or shots fired in anger. The level of fighting was low during the holidays, the VC out of sight.

Within a few days after New Year's, however, helicopters came in and lifted the company off for an assault on a village west of Duc Pho near the mountains. "It was," remembers one member of the company, "a breeze. I think we fired a couple of shots at things stirring in the bush. But that was all. We didn't really see any VC that we could call VC for sure. We went into a couple of villes, passed out some candy and rations to the people and then moved out. Then the choppers came back and lifted us off for the LZ. Some of us thought then that if that's war, it's going to be a breeze."

In the next few weeks, there were daily missions out from the fire-base. Civilians were rounded up in what were considered hostile hamlets and moved to resettlement camps. Hootches were burned. But that was about all. The company, the whole brigade, had been lucky so far.

New orders arrived on January 26, 1968. The three rifle companies and an artillery battery under command of Colonel Barker—the composition of Task Force Barker—were moved forty miles north to what was called Landing Zone Dottie, a fire-base northeast of the city of Quang Ngai, right in the heart of Indian Country with the VC all around.

At LZ Dottie, the men lived in underground bunkers to protect them from possible VC rocket attacks, something that could happen on any night without warning. The LZ, as with all LZ's, was surrounded by a maze of barbed concertina wire to which, at night, anti-personnel Claymore mines were strung to blow up VC sappers if they tried to get through the wire. Also at night, small patrols were sent to move about the area just outside the wire to hold back any VC assaults.

"Shit, man," one soldier recalls, "we were scared all the time. You never knew when the dinks were gonna come in. Christ, I mean, one time I went to this demonstration at a fire-base near Chu Lai. They had this *cheiu hoi* [former VC who have come in and joined the ARVN] showing how the VC come through the wire. This little dink stripped down to just this little cloth so, he says, he could feel the wire on his skin if he touched it. Then he squirmed through that wire faster than I could run it. And he apologized. I mean, he says that if it was night it would have taken him a couple of seconds longer. This dink, he tells us that the VC sometimes they just come in through the wire and don't do nothing. I mean, they do it night after night. Then they go out into the jungle and build themselves a model of the LZ and practice coming through the wire so's they'll know how when they decide to attack. Sometimes when they come through, of course, they come with explosives and blow up everything around. So you never know. I mean, man, I was scared shitless all the time at the LZ. We all were."

But scared or not, there was plenty to do; there was a war to fight. Task Force Barker, as part of the larger Operation Muscatine which was searching and destroying VC througout southern I Corps, was assigned an area of operations covering a ten by fifteen mile rectangle northeast of Quang Ngai city. It took in the Son Tinh district, including the village of Son My, as well as the Binh Son district and others adjoining Highway Number One on east to the sea.

The area was theoretically under the jurisdiction of the

ARVN Second Division headquartered in Quang Ngai. But there was little communication between the ARVN and the Americans, and the Americans acted as though the ARVN was not even there. This situation was to lead, two years later during an investigation of the massacre, to the charge by Senator Tran Van Don, a former general, Defense Minister, one of the leaders of the coup that overthrew Diem and now leader of the opposition to the Thieu government in Saigon, that the massacre "was much more of a Vietnamese mistake. Of course the Americans helped. But it shows the lack of coordination between the two commands. The operation was under the command of the South Vietnamese Army Second Division so the Vietnamese had more responsibility."

Until Task Force Barker arrived at LZ Dottie, the allied force operating freely within the area had been the Koreans. Of the Koreans there had been universal fear. The people of the area considered them merciless, ready to shoot at anything and certain to take extreme vengeance on anyone who shot at them.

In a refugee camp outside Quang Ngai, I met a thirty-year-old woman, Nguyen Thi Bot, her three small children clustered around her. She is from An Ky hamlet in the village of Son Hai, just north of Son My village, at the mouth of the Cho Mai River. The Koreans, she says, came and shot up her hamlet one day, killing eighteen people, including her mother, father and sister-in-law.

A man near by, in this charcoal-smelling hootch, nods. He, it seems, was the deputy village chief of Son Hai, and he lived in the sub-hamlet of Ky Bac in the hamlet of An Ky. "The ROK's," he says, "came to my area and the VC were there then and they contacted the VC that day. The Koreans had some casualties from the VC."

When was this?

"In 1967."

Then what happened?

"Then some of the people will be killed when the Koreans come back."

You expected this?

"It happened. Everyone knew what happens with the Koreans. The Koreans came back and the VC were there at that time. The VC mixed with the people in a crowd in the hamlet. The VC were in the middle of the people. So the Koreans fired into the people and some people, about twenty, were killed that day. My own mother and father, sixty-seven years old and seventy-two years old, and my aunt-in-law were killed in that Korean invasion."

When was that?

"In October of 1967."

How do you feel about it?

"That is war. That is what happened. My own mother and father were killed, but Son Hai was not secure then. It is not secure now, either."

In January of 1968, Task Force Barker and the Americans moved in and the Koreans moved out. The three infantry companies settled into LZ Dottie, the task force headquarters, while the artillery battery took over nearby LZ Uptight from which it could direct its fire anywhere over the area under Barker's command.

The mission of Task Force Barker was simple and direct, no different from the missions of the hundreds of other similar American units operating out of LZ's all over Vietnam. The area, as Medina notes, "was a permanent free-fire zone." In essence, this meant that any Americans operating within it had, basically, a license to kill and any Vietnamese living within it had a license to be killed. The men were told that the VC, the communists, had had free reign in the region for twenty or twenty-five years, that all the civilians in the territory had been warned and so knew its status as a free-fire zone and that, therefore, they could fall under fire at any time. The people living in the villages and hamlets, Medina says and the company believed, "had all been moved at one time or another."

Though all the Americans in LZ Dottie, as all American soldiers entering Vietnam, had heard the standard lecture about respecting the traditions and customs of the people, and been told to try as best they could to protect and defend civilians caught in VC areas, to take special care not to fire at or harm unarmed civilians who were acting in a peaceful and non-threatening manner, such advice was forgotten almost as soon as it was given. For what was also told, and followed more closely, was that American soldiers had every right, and in fact a duty, to fire when fired upon and to act in an appropriate manner when under attack or when threatened.

"How the hell," asks one young soldier, "can you tell when some dink is just going about his business or when maybe he's a VC ready to throw down on you?"

Three days after arriving at LZ Dottie, Charley Company ran into its first trouble in Vietnam. On a routine patrol in the northern sector of its area, well to the north of Son My, one young private stumbled across a booby trap. He was slightly wounded, but the explosion and the sight of a friend down on the ground crying in pain for help shook everyone up. "Right then," a young sergeant recalls, "we knew we were in Indian country, that this wasn't going to be no picnic."

And, in fact, two nights later all over Vietnam, all hell broke loose. The major VC-NVA assault of the war had begun. The Tet Offensive of 1968 was on.

Almost simultaneously that night, VC and NVA forces fell on thirty-six of South Vietnam's forty-four provincial capitals. And with the sound of guns, American illusions about the course

93

of the war, that it was moving ever upward and onward to victory, were riddled.

In Saigon, the VC moved right into the heart of the city. They over-ran part of the American Embassy compound only a couple of blocks from the Gia Long Palace, the presidential residence. The mammoth Ton Son Nhut airbase on the outskirts of Saigon was under such steady rocket attack and small arms fire that the planes were unable to use it for several days. The VC occupied Saigon's twin Chinese city, Cholon, for more than two weeks. They were driven out only by the far superior American fire power, including air assaults and artillery. But when finally they retreated, underground and from Saigon, they had proved that even the heart of the capital was not safe. And they had done more. For in the minds of the people of Saigon more than a few questions had been raised about the concern of the government and of the Americans for the safety and well-being of the ordinary Vietnamese citizen. When the battle for Cholon was over, 133,000 residents of Saigon found themselves homeless, their houses destroyed by the artillery and air strikes of the Americans.

What happened in Saigon was repeated in city after city, provincial capital after provincial capital all over the country. The VC and the NVA managed to penetrate into the hearts of most of them, fighting pitched battles with the Americans when forced to retreat and, in the process, causing the virtual destruction of many of these cities—destruction which could be blamed on the Americans, since it was their bombs and artillery shells which had done the damage in the battle to dislodge the VC. At Ben Tre, for example, when the action ended the American officer who led the counter-attack declared, "It became necessary to destroy the town to save it."

The major all-out attacks during Tet were aimed at Saigon and at the ancient royal capital of Vietnam, Hue, in the northern section of South Vietnam. Both the VC and the NVA regulars took part in the assault. They smashed and routed the ARVN defenders, took control of Hue and held it for more than three weeks. When the Americans counter-attacked, they fought battles from house to house, leaving havoc and destruction in their wake as they slowly retreated. Again, the havoc and destruction were in no small measure the result of American bombardments in an effort to dislodge the VC from Hue. Almost every weapon in the American arsenal in Vietnam was brought to bear on the city—bombs, rockets, napalm, naval artillery, nausea gas, small arms.

When the VC and the NVA finally abandoned the city of Hue on February 24, with the Americans at last in control of the ancient Citadel, more than 70 per cent of the homes in the city were rubble, perhaps 120,000 of the 145,000 residents were refugees and nearly 4,000 civilians were dead.

The VC had conducted a blood-thirsty vengeance in Hue. They had, while in control of the city, killed and interred in mass graves somewhere between 3,000 and 5,000 people—most of them political opponents, potential opponents, government employees, teachers and the like. Thus when the city was finally recaptured, not only was it wreckage, not only were its people homeless and comotose, but its educated ruling class and those upon whom the government relied for loyalty had been slaughtered.

What the VC and the NVA did in Hue must certainly stand as one of the great atrocities of the war. It was deliberate massacre of selected victims regardless of age or sex.

The VC did not neglect Quang Ngai, either, to the south of Task Force Barker's fire base, LZ Dottie. In wave after wave they penetrated the city, reaching almost to its center until pushed back by the Americans and the ARVN Second Division stationed there. Near the center of Quang Ngai are two hospitals just across the street from each other. One is military, guarded and surrounded by bunkers, barbed wire and armed men. The other is a relatively unprotected civilian facility. On several of their forays in Quang Ngai, the VC, avoiding the military hospital, attacked the civilian hospital, raced through its corridors and shot bed-ridden patients, nurses and doctors before being driven back by the forces across the street.

At first the Americans tended to belittle the offensive. President Johnson described it then—and does even today—as "a complete failure." General William Westmoreland, then the American commander in Vietnam, thought it only "a diversionary effort." But when the scope and the magnitude of the fighting became apparent, the American Army in Vietnam talked only of the successes of American forces in repelling the VC and the NVA and of the heavy losses incurred by the enemy. Claiming that 84,000 enemy troops were taking part in the Tet offensive, the Army said that by February 11, or two weeks after the fighting began, more than 32,000 had been killed. By March 1, when the offensive finally came to an end, the American claims of VC-NVA deaths had mounted to 45,000, or more than half of those supposedly engaged in the fighting.

It seems evident that like so many other claims by the United States about the war in Vietnam, the estimates of enemy losses during the Tet offensive were grossly exaggerated and overly optimistic. No one will ever know just what the losses were. But it is evident that though the VC and the NVA were hit hard and did suffer large casualties in the fighting, they were far from finished in Vietnam. Nevertheless, when the all-out battles of Tet were over, the level of combat in Vietnam fell sharply. American troops once again took the offensive in an intensified fashion in an attempt, they thought, to totally decimate the already depleted strength of the VC and the NVA.

Tet roared all around but Charley Company and Task Force

Barker were in the eye of the hurricane. Though the sounds of the fighting in Quang Ngai city to the south, and the booming thunder of the jets on the attack could be heard by the company all during the offensive, it was more a distant spectator than an active participant.

Soon after the VC erupted from the countryside like molten lava from a thousand hidden volcanos, Medina got orders to move Charley Company from LZ Dottie south to a hill labeled on the army maps as Hill 102 and called Nui Dong De, over-looking the Ham Giang River to the south and highway Number One a little way west.

Hill 102, or Nui Dong De, is several miles northwest of Son My village, located within Son Long village and separated from Son My by a number of ridges and hills. But Medina was later to tell one reporter that the hill overlooked the "Pinkville" area and the northern approaches to Quang Ngai city. Since Son My and all its hamlets and sub-hamlets—My Lai, Tu Cung and the rest—are some distance east-north-east of Quang Ngai, Medina's statement as to where he was must be considered inaccurate. But this is not surprising. Whenever Americans gave me more than one reference point in locating where they were at specific times, a check of the maps usually found that they were wrong by a considerable distance. It is doubtful whether Medina or any other member of the company ever knew exactly where the company was at any particular moment; this is not surprising for few Americans in Vietnam, unfamiliar with the terrain as they are and convinced that one hamlet looks pretty much like any other hamlet, are ever exactly certain about their location.

From this new outpost on Hill 102, blocking traffic—and, supposedly, reinforcements for the VC—into and out of Quang Ngai city both along the highway and along the river valley, Charley Company spent a part of Tet. Soon after it took up its positions, a group of 200 or 300 Vietnamese carrying arms was spotted moving northeast out of Quang Ngai which had come under fierce attack the previous night. The group, with women and children in its midst, was undoubtedly VC. Medina radioed for artillery fire to blast the moving column. But foul-ups at the artillery base and then red tape to get clearance from Americal headquarters in Chu Lai consumed several hours. By the time the artillery commander radioed back to Medina that he was ready to direct his fire, the column had vanished down the river valley.

Then the company settled in to the steady—and terrifying—grind of war in Vietnam. Operating from Hill 102 and then back at LZ Dottie, there were the daily patrols down muddy paths, across dripping rice paddies, never sure what might be buried in the mud, or what hidden wire might be tripped as one stepped unawares, or what sudden fury filled with spikes might crash from the trees, or into what hidden pit dotted with sharpened bamboo spikes one might tumble.

Still Charley Company was the lucky company. It rarely met the enemy and seemed to be able to find its way around mine fields and booby traps without trouble. So it suffered few casualties.

In these early days of combat, the men began to solidify their previously formed and now lasting impressions of their officers and sergeants. Medina, for one, seemed totally impervious to danger. In fact, he seemed almost to be searching for it, to test the courage of his men and of himself. At the same time, he seemed totally dedicated to the welfare of his own men, concerned about them, grieving when one of them was wounded, concerned that they be fed well, have shelter and ammunition. It was, one of the men remembers, "like he was some kind of hen taking care of her brood, if you know what I mean. If we was out in the field, one platoon going one way and another going a different way and there was some shots, then Medina'd be on the field phone right away, wanting to know what the shooting was about, if anybody was hurt, if reinforcements were needed, that kind of thing. He had to know everything that was happening everywhere in the company."

But if Medina was concerned about his own men, those who served under him noticed that he seemed utterly oblivious to the Vietnamese. On occasions when the company entered a hamlet and all was peaceful, Medina seemed bored, anxious to get moving after he had posed a few questions to the village chiefs through his interpreter, and there would be a look of weary impatience when his soldiers passed out cigarettes and canned fruit to the villagers. "I mean," one of his soldiers says, "he didn't ever talk about the gooks. He didn't call them any names, just didn't seem to care one way or another about them. I mean, it seemed to a lot of us that he sometimes didn't ever know they were there, didn't pay any attention to them, didn't know they were people. Except, of course, when some guy got hit, then Medina'd get real angry and talk about how we'd get ours back at them. That's all he ever called them where I heard him— them. Now don't get me wrong. He was a damn good officer. You were convinced you were going to be about as safe as a soldier can be with Medina around. Sure he was looking for action, but you felt he wasn't going to go throwing somebody's life away just for a couple of medals, for a chance to be a hero and get a promotion."

No matter what the men did to Vietnamese civilians—and they were not usually very gentle with them—no one can remember ever being chastised by Medina or any of the other officers in Charley Company. In fact, there is only one occasion that anyone can remember when a soldier in Charley Company was brought to task for his treatment of a Vietnamese civilian. On one mission into a hamlet, three soldiers allegedly raped a young Vietnamese girl. When he found out about it, the company's Vietnamese interpreter went to Medina and angrily threatened to report the rape to higher authorities unless Medina did something about it. When members of the company heard about this, they threatened to ambush the interpreter, but this plan was dropped. However, the interpreter's report to Medina was acted upon. None of the men was court-martialed, but one of them was disciplined and reduced in rank.

From this and other events, the men in Charley Company felt that Medina would back them against the Vietnamese any time, that he was behind them all the way.

Calley was something different. About the best that anyone had to say for him was the summation by one corporal in his platoon: "He wasn't the best officer in the world, but then he wasn't the worst one, either."

There were others, however, who weren't quite so sure of that. Some thought him more than a little Napoleonic, using the war and his rank for his own self-glorification, for his own self-importance. It was his opportunity to be big and often he attempted to prove himself even bigger than life. And there were some who saw things slightly off-center about him, though they find it difficult to say exactly what and how. "I never felt easy when Calley was leading us on a patrol and the rest of the company, say another officer or Medina, wasn't around," one of his privates said. "It was like he was all wound up tight, just waiting to bust loose. And when he busted, everyone around him was going to be hit by the pieces. It was just a feeling, like there were only a couple of times he did anything to make you sure that your feelings were right. And I wasn't the only guy felt this, the only guy who was waiting for the day Calley went. Like he was a little guy, see, all puffed up, trying to make himself bigger and taller than anybody else. I guess maybe you can only do that for so long and then look out, man."

There were a number of men who pointed to an episode early

in February when they were looking for some concrete evidence to back their then-vague feelings about Calley. According to James Bergthold, for one, one afternoon Calley deliberately murdered a Vietnamese civilian without any provocation. The platoon was on a routine patrol when Bergthold brought in a Vietnamese civilian, about sixty years old, whom he had just discovered in a paddy. "I brought the guy in," he said. "He was standing in a field all by himself. I brought him in, and the lieutenant asked him questions and then threw him in a well and shot him in the head. He never said why he did it."

But if there was uncertainty about Calley's balance, most of the men thought they had a steadying and modifying influence in Sergeant Mitchell. "He was regular army," one soldier in his squad says approvingly. "He wouldn't take no shit from anyone. He was a tough son of bitch and I think that got on the asses of a couple of the white boys from the south who had to take his orders. But an officer give him an order, it was done right then. And when he gave an order it had better get done and no fucking around. Nobody wanted Mitchell to be chewing their ass for them. You felt he knew where he was going and why all the time."

The task force was really bloodied for the first time on February 5, and at last the men realized that there was an enemy out there and he could and would fight back. That morning, the choppers took the task force southeast toward the village of Son My to interdict elements of the 48th Local Force Battalion which was on the move during the Tet offensive. While two companies—Able Company and Bravo Company—moved in to engage the VC in combat, Charley Company set up a blocking ambush at a small stream to the north. Able and Bravo made contact and for a time a savage battle was fought, with intense small arms fire and rockets tearing up the landscape. As the fighting swirled through the countryside, Charley Company suddenly found itself engaged, and shots were fired back and forth for a short time. Then the VC faded back into the landscape and the Americans pulled back to their fire base. There had been casualties on both sides. One man in Charley Company had been killed, the company's first battle death after little more than a month in the Vietnam war zone.

The regular daily grind of the war in Vietnam continued. What is that war for the men who fight it? The patrols in squad, platoon and company strength move out from the fire base into the villages and hamlets, into the thickets and the groves, through the rice paddies, down mud and dirt trails. This is the nature of the war for the American "grunts"—the name derisively given themselves by the infantry. There are no headlines; few battles are fought or won. The enemy is rarely seen or met. But the Americans are always conscious that he is somewhere around.

Fear always accompanies these patrols, the terror that the next field may be littered with mines, that a booby trap may be just ahead on the trail, that a VC ambush is around the next bend. And with this fear comes the growing anger and growing hatred of the Vietnamese, all Vietnamese. When a casualty is taken, there is usually no one around at whom to unleash the mounting fury. Frustration grows at the inability to find anyone on whom to vent one's anger and leads to the insensate desire to hit out at something, to get a measure of revenge.

More and more as these daily patrols went on without end, the men in Task Force Barker grew to hate the dirty war they were part of, a war where everything and nothing was the enemy and fair game, where trouble could come from anyone or anything. And they began to take casualties now and again, here and there. Moving down a trail one afternoon somewhere in their district (no one is sure exactly where, as most of the men were never really sure where they were except that they were somewhere in Vietnam), a mine suddenly exploded. Three men went down, one of them dead. Just off the trail, hidden in the brush, was a fifteen year old girl, her hand still on the detonator of the mine. Simultaneously, four or five soldiers fired. The girl fell over the detonator, riddled with bullets, dead.

Another day, in mid-February, one of the companies in Task Force Barker stumbled into a VC ambush. According to a later report in the Pacific edition of Stars and Stripes, it "fought its way out . . . leaving 80 enemy dead." But the company did not come off unscathed itself. The official reports said that one American had been killed and four wounded; according to men in the task force, however, their casualties had been considerably understated.

Yet Charley Company was the lucky company in Task Force Barker. It had taken relatively few wounded and killed and most of its patrols have been relatively uneventful. Medina was chafing over the lack of action, because, as rifleman Richard Pendleton remembers, "he wanted us to be the best, always out in the field, he wanted us to stay out more, to kill more people."

They had been to war, though, and little things happened on every patrol which brought this home crushingly to them, the realization of the kind of war they were in. Also brought home to a few was their uncertainty about some of their leaders.

Michael Bernhardt has several such memories. He recalls the time, soon after Charley Company arrived at LZ Dottie, when the first platoon was on patrol. Racing across a field ahead of them was a Vietnamese woman. Calley turned toward Bernhardt and ordered him to stop her. Bernhardt yelled out, "Dong lai! Dong lai!"—the Vietnamese for halt or stop. The woman ignored the command and kept going, disappearing into some trees across the field. Calley was furious, Bernhardt says, and raged at him that if in the future a Vietnamese disobeyed an order to stop that Vietnamese was to be shot.

Other things, little things mainly, disturbed Bernhardt and a few others. But when one asks other members of the company about them, they nod in remembrance but dismiss them as nothing either out of the ordinary or disturbing.

Things like these happened almost daily on missions. Another woman runs across the field. Across her shoulders is the traditional long bamboo pole with baskets balanced at either end. The cry of "Dong lai!" She ignores it. She must be VC. Some of the men aim and shoot. An examination of her body and the baskets reveals only merchandise bought at the nearby market. She was not VC, at least not on the outward evidence.

Moving down a dirt road, the platoon spots a woman and a small child in the near distance, in the midst of a field. There is a break, the men fall out and rest by the side of the road. Several of the soldiers walk casually across the field to the woman and child. They grab her, throw her to the ground, pull up her skirts and then, one by one, rape her while the child stands by screaming, wriggling in the grasp of one of the soldiers. When they are finished, one of the men takes his rifle and casually shoots the woman through the head. He turns and just as casually kills the child.

The platoon moves along the outskirts of another hamlet. A couple of shots are fired from inside the perimeter of the hamlet, among the row of thatched hootches. Over the field telephone, Calley calls for air support against this hostile hamlet. Soon helicopter gunships appear in the air overhead and strafe the settlement repeatedly with cannon and machinegun fire. They leave and there is silence amidst the smoke and flames of the ruined settlement. The platoon cautiously enters the ruins. On the path just inside the first row of houses there are the bodies of two small children, ripped apart by the strafing.

Another hamlet. Some of the men see a young Vietnamese girl. They grab her and pull her inside the nearest hootch. There

are screams and cries from inside and then silence. Soon the men
come walking out, satisfied.

The people have gathered in the center of another hamlet,
smiling and greeting the Americans, milling around them while
cigarettes, gum, canned fruits are passed out. A couple of the
men wander casually about the settlement. They go into one
hootch and emerge carrying a number of trinkets, relics and
family heirlooms and start to rejoin the rest of the platoon. An
old man breaks away from the group and trots after them. He
bows his head, folds his hands and with a humble, obsequious
smile murmurs words in Vietnamese to them and points with
anguish at the souvenirs they are carrying away. It was his
hootch and he would like his possessions returned. He grows
tiresome and one of the soldiers turns and without a thought
shoots him.

Day after day the dirty incidents of this kind, in this kind of
war, mount. Almost every day there is something else, some
other casual depredation by the American GI's, done without
thought, with no real meaning for them. They have now come
to look at Vietnamese as some sub-human species who live only
by the grace of the Americans; to kill them is no more a crime
than to spray DDT on an annoying insect; they have no rights,
to property, to life, to anything; their lives, their bodies, everything they have and own is at the disposal of the Americans, to
take or leave as they will, without thought. To the Americans, it
is meaningless, rarely done with malice, for there is no thought
that what is being done is being done to human beings with
desires and rights of their own. The value of human life, of
Vietnamese civilian life grew cheaper and cheaper. The fear of
these Vietnamese and the hatred of them grew ever stronger in
the Americans, though it was depersonalized. And something
else grew too. The veneer of civilization, as it must in any war,
was banished and in its place came the face of the killer. In

dehumanizing and depersonalizing the Vietnamese, the Americans had themselves become depersonalized and dehumanized, had become vultures on the land, scavengers in a strange country, leaving in their wake nothing but death and destruction, and the hatred of those they had wronged. And like some horrible never-ending chain, the sensed hatred and fear of the Vietnamese toward Americans was translated into even deeper hatred and fear of Americans toward Vietnamese. And so the mask of the killer was donned. For some of the Americans in Charley Company, as in any company, the mask was donned to cover an inner, deeper disaster which had to be buried. It was the horror which came with the realization that they hated, in addition to everything else, and feared children, that they could kill children.

Charley Company's luck began to change. The odds swung, as they obviously would. Early on the morning of February 25, the company was lifted from LZ Dottie to the northern corner of its sector, near the village of Lac Son in the Bin Son district, only a few miles below the border between Quang Ngai and Quang Tin provinces. It was to have been only a normal sweep through the area, searching for VC and moving through nearby hamlets to question the civilians. If VC had been found in one of the hamlets, the hootches would have been burned, the hamlet totally destroyed. But then there was nothing new in destroying hamlets. That had become an everyday occurrence for the company. As one soldier later said, "We were supposed to be on search-and-destroy missions, but we did a hell of lot more destroying than we did searching."

But this turned out to be more than just the normal operation.

About noon, with Calley's first platoon in the lead, the company began to edge across a field just south of Lac Son. Suddenly a mine went off. Another and another and another exploded here and there in the field. "Every time somebody made a move, he'd go up," Bernhardt recalls.

They had walked into the middle of a field laced with land mines. Everyone froze. Some men began to scream in panic and fear. Some, in utter terror, totally lost control and tried to flee, but within a few steps they were lifted off the ground by another explosion. The field echoed with screams and everywhere there was blood and pieces of human flesh and bones. Six men died in that field that afternoon, and twelve were wounded. And more were so filled with terror and unthinkable horror that for days thereafter they were unable to function, woke up in the night with the sweat of fear covering them, screaming from the nightmares of remembrance.

One of those who died to the mines of Lac Son was nineteen year old Bobby Wilson. His friend Paul Meadlo would later remember him as "a damn good buddy," and would become determined to gain revenge for his friend on those who had planted the mines, the invisible enemy.

In the midst of the panic that day, Medina showed the coolness, bravery and concern for his men that had come to be expected. While everyone else, including other officers, remained frozen, afraid to move or breathe, Medina, treading carefully, threaded his way through the mine field and recovered several of the wounded, including his radio man James Vanleer, and led the rest of the men to safety. As he was accomplishing this, a mine went off and he was slightly wounded. It was not, though, serious enough to require hospitalization, needing only minor dressing. For his action that day at Lac Son, Medina was awarded the Silver Star, the army's third highest medal.

The war began to heat up for Task Force Barker and for Charley Company. Several intense fire-fights took place within its operating zone. Several men were killed and more were wounded. There was no way to tell when a fire fight might break out. The morning would start as usual, with a routine search-and-destroy mission scheduled. But sometime during the day, the VC would be waiting, the blood would be spilled on the land. Day after day it was the same thing. There was no relief. It was days out on patrol, many nights bivouacked in some field or in some hamlet, the men sleeping only from fatigue, the sentries constantly on the alert. Then it would be back to the fire base, back to LZ Dottie, back to the bunkers with no amusements, no nights off for a drink or a girl. Just the grinding fear and hate and frustration of war.

By mid-March, the task force had been in the field about two and a half months without a break. Though there had been casualties, a number of men dead and wounded, the casualties had not been excessive, about normal for such a company of infantry in such a station. And the company's strength was not too seriously depleted, down to a little over a hundred men. But the grinding frustration of war, the inability to strike back at a visible enemy had taken their toll of morale. This had become a real problem. Even Medina noted that morale in Charley Company was "not at its highest."

Then word came that the opportunity to strike back at the enemy in what might well be a major engagement had arrived. Medina was told that his company and the two others in Task Force Barker would be taking on the VC's 48th Local Force Battalion at one of its major bases and would have the opportunity to destroy the VC group which had over the years earned the reputation as one of the toughest and most elusive in Vietnam.

Information had come to Army intelligence both from its own operators in the field and from friendly Vietnamese that the VC 48th had been making a base in Son My village, in the hamlet the local people called My Lai. Knowing how Americans were bewildered by Vietnamese names, it is doubtful if the Vietnamese informants had narrowed the location any further, to the specific sub-hamlet within My Lai—that is My Khe. And they would have hesitated even further to narrow it down since there was another hamlet in the village with the same name, My Khe. So, as far as the Americans then knew, the center of the VC was at My Lai hamlet.

But what the Vietnamese could not have known was that on the American military maps there was more than one My Lai. There were six of them. Where the VC were, My Khe, was the sub-hamlet the Americans called My Lai (1) and on the maps it was shaded in pink. The Americans called it "Pinkville."

The operation would be a direct attack: the task force would go to Pinkville and assault the VC on their home ground, destroying the battalion, the hamlet and all the other hamlets within the village. What had been considered a VC sanctuary would be no more, and the civilians who had been helping the VC within that sanctuary would be forcibly moved and relocated in "protected" camps where they would be safe from VC and/or would no longer be able to help this enemy.

On March 15, a new commander arrived to take over the brigade. He was Colonel Oran K. Henderson. He was briefed on the forthcoming operation by his executive officer, Colonel Barker.

Then Barker and Medina got into a helicopter at LZ Dottie and flew down to the area around Son My. They did not fly directly overhead, not wishing to alert the supposedly waiting VC to what was coming. Instead, they circled the area and then returned to LZ Dottie, to prepare the onslaught the next morning.

At dusk that evening, Medina gathered his company together at the fire base to brief them on the operation for the next day. "I told them," he says, "that the intelligence reports indicated that the 48th VC Battalion was in the village and the intelligence reports indicated that there would be no women and children in the village, that they would have gone to market."

His company, Medina told the more than one hundred soldiers sitting in front of him that night in the fading twilight, would have the job of spearheading the operation and of engaging in the main action the following morning. Company A would land to the north and set up blocking positions to prevent the VC from escaping the trap. Company B would be set down to the east and eventually link up with the other two companies.

In the attack, Medina told the men, the objective would be to engage and destroy the VC, to burn the houses in the village, to blow up bunkers and tunnels, to kill the livestock and, if possible, to destroy the crops, and, if any civilian stragglers were found, to shove them out of the area.

"The object," Medina stressed, "was to destroy the village so that the 48th VC would have to move."

But certain that the following day would bring heavy fighting —both because of the orders and because of the intelligence reports he had seen—Medina was more than slightly nervous and he was certain that the men in his company felt the same way. So Medina spent much of that evening priming them for action. "My objective was to fire them up to get them ready to go in there. I did not give any instructions as to what to do with women and children in the village." He did not, he says, because he did not think there would be any women and children there.

James Bergthold remembers that during the briefing "the captain told us—we weren't given any orders to shoot—that if we saw anyone at all they might be carrying weapons, so be careful."

Others, however, remember the briefing in a different way. Richard Pendleton says, "He told us there were Viet Cong in the village and we should kill them before they kill us."

Bernhardt says that the captain ordered that "the village and the occupants were to be destroyed." Medina claimed, according to Bernhardt, that "they were all VC and there were no innocent civilians in the area."

And Vernardo Simpson remembers that the orders were to "kill or burn down anything in sight."

Whatever the orders—and it is almost certain that they were to kill everything there, since Medina was convinced there would be no civilians in the area—the mood of the men for the next morning was set that evening. "Captain Medina told us we might get a chance to revenge the deaths of our fellow GI's," says Charles West who had just been raised to squad leader when Sergeant Cox was killed by a booby trap. "I think what we heard," he adds, "put fear into a lot of our hearts. We thought we'd run into heavy resistance. He was telling us that here was the enemy, the enemy that had been killing our buddies. This was going to be our first real live battle, and we had made up our minds we were going in and with whatever means possible wipe them out."

At dawn the next morning, March 16, 1968, eight UH-1-E troop-carrying helicopters arrived at LZ Dottie and began to ferry the men of Task Force Barker southeast toward their "first real live battle."

PART THREE

One Morning in the War

F OR Nguyen Van Danh, the deputy sub-hamlet chief of My Hoi, it had been a night of such pleasurable excitement that he had had trouble going to sleep. For the first time in four years he had seen his own house, had slept under his own roof, and he had luxuriated in the feeling of being home again. His neighbors who had stayed in the sub-hamlet all those years had come to welcome him back with the others who had returned the previous night. They had sat under the stars and talked long before going to bed. Some of what they had said had left him with an uneasy feeling. The government's claim that the village was now pacified, that the VC had departed, had been driven out, was rejected by those who had stayed. ARVN troops had patrolled the area on a few occasions, fought minor skirmishes with the VC, but VC were still only a little over a klick to the north in My Khe, and the VC still came to My Hoi whenever it wanted to, with little opposition.

But, still, it was good to be home. As he woke that bright sunny morning, Danh realized that it was late; he had finally gone to sleep very late and had slept longer than he had planned. He had meant to be up early and just walk through the village and the paddies, walk down to the river, just enjoy being back.

Danh is uncertain exactly what woke him. Perhaps it was the sound. For in the distance, a little way to the west, he thought he heard the concussion of bombs and rockets, the sound of machine gun fire. At first he thought it was just his imagination. He went to the door and outside, peering toward the sounds in the west. And he could make out, hovering, helicopters. And he could see smoke and sudden bright flashes of shells exploding.

Nguyen To was at work in his rice paddy just outside Xom Lang before seven that morning. He was worried and the feel of soil and grain in his hands, the sun on his back, alleviated his concerns for the moment. He had gone early to the paddy just for that purpose, so he would not have to think about his troubles and to enjoy the paddy and the earth and the sun, for he was sure that he did not have much longer to enjoy them.

Two of his sons were off somewhere, he did not know where, fighting with the VC. His other three sons, younger, were still at home, but one of them was talking about leaving, not to join his brothers in the VC but to go west to Quang Ngai and join the ARVN. His two younger sons were still too small—only ten and fourteen—for politics and the war.

Just a few days before some ARVN had come into the hamlet during the day. They had come to his home to talk to him about his sons, about his own feelings. And from their manner toward him, from the tone of their voices, he knew he was suspected of harboring VC sympathies, of being a secret VC. And he was certain that even though he was sixty-two, he would be arrested by the government soon and taken to prison. "I did not like the government," he insists today, after having spent most of the two years since that March day in a government prison as a VC sympathizer, "but I was not VC. My two sons were VC, but I had no interest in politics."

As he worked, To thought he heard sharp clattering sounds overhead. He looked up and saw an American helicopter hovering over Xom Lang. It circled the settlement two or three times and then turned north and disappeared. A few moments later he heard a loud thud, a KAPLOW that shook the ground. The first shells had fallen on Xom Lang.

Breakfast was just being served at Mr. Sam's brick house. The immediate family and relatives and in-laws had crowded into the house and Mr. Sam's wife was spooning the morning rice from the cooking pot into each bowl. Ngo Ngo Thininh, Mr. Sam's nineteen year old daughter-in-law, her husband away fighting for the ARVN, remembers that her four-year-old brother was standing near the pot. His bowl had just been filled and he was about to dip his spoon into the rice.

The first shells hit just outside the house and everything shook and reverberated. She saw the bowl and the spoon drop from her brother's hands and shatter on the floor. Mr. Sam immediately ordered everyone into the bunkers outside for shelter until the shelling stopped.

For Nguyen Chi this Saturday was to have been market day. With many things to do at home, she rose early, intending to get to the market at Chau Thanh quickly and be back home with her husband and three young children before noon. They were just rising when she left the house and started down the road toward the market. Moving rapidly along the side of the road she paid little attention to what was happening above and around her until suddenly she heard a bomb explode with a loud thud behind her, from the direction of Xom Lang.

"I turned around," she remembers. "I saw them exploding in my hamlet. So I ran to a near house. It was right near the main road where I was walking. The people in the house took me down to the bunker and we all hid there. As we were going into the bunker, we saw the choppers coming overhead. One of them landed in a rice paddy near the road about one klick from where I was."

Later, when the sound of the bombs had stopped, she came out of the bunker, but quickly ducked back in when she saw

American soldiers moving toward the hamlet, shooting. She stayed out just long enough, however, to look in the direction of her home which was in the first row of houses. She saw "GI burning my house and my cow house, too."

It was just about seven in the morning when the first shells began to rain on Xom Lang that March 16th. Those who were still at home—most of the people in the sub-hamlet, for it was still early and many of them were just beginning breakfast—quickly sought shelter in their family bunkers. Almost every house had its bunker dug into the ground nearby. The VC when they had arrived had forced the people to build them, and from friends in other hamlets they had heard enough tales to know that in case of a bombardment, a bunker was one of the few hopes of survival. So each family dug its own.

The shells continued to thud into the ground and explode, destroying houses and gouging deep craters for about twenty minutes. The artillery barrage marched up and down the hamlet and the area around it, preparing the landing zone for the troop-carrying helicopters. Overhead, helicopter gunships hovered without any opposition, pounding the hamlet and the ground around it with rockets and machine gun fire.

When the artillery finally stopped, there was a momentary silence, made louder by the sudden absence of exploding high-explosives, and then the air filled with the ear-shattering clatter of the helicopters beginning to settle into the rice paddies and fields at the western edge of Xom Lang.

Captain Ernest Medina was in the lead chopper, watching the artillery and the gunships level Xom Lang. He "could see the smoke and flash of artillery" as the settlement was ripped apart. Then his helicopter settled into a paddy about a hundred and fifty meters west. Immediately the door gunners strafed the surrounding countryside with machine gun fire in case there happened to be VC waiting among the growing rice and brush.

As far as Medina could tell there was no return fire. "My instant impression," he says, "was that I didn't hear the familiar crackle of rifle bullets zinging over my head."

Accompanied by his radio operator and other company aides, Medina clambered down from the helicopter and rushed across the paddy to the edge of a small graveyard just at the edge of Xom Lang. Still there was no return fire, and all around him the other choppers were settling to the ground and the men of Company C were pouring through the doors, firing toward the houses as they emerged. It seemed to have occurred to no one at that moment that the lack of return fire might mean that this was not the hamlet where the VC was centered, that this was not "Pinkville."

But Medina did note the lack of armed resistance. He radioed back to the tactical operations center at LZ Dottie that the landing had been smooth and that his men had come under no fire. "I reported the LZ is cold. Immediately thereafter the helicopter pilot broke in and reported, 'Negative, negative, negative. LZ is hot. You are receiving small arms fire.'"

This was the only report that morning of opposition. And it is more than likely that the pilot thought the firing of the American troops moving in toward Xom Lang indicated that small arms were being shot back from the settlement.

Though Medina could neither see nor hear any return fire from the houses, he quickly passed the word to the leaders of his three platoons, two of them blocking access to Xom Lang, or My Lai (4) as the Americans had it on their maps, and to Calley's first platoon advancing on the settlement itself. "I told them to move with extreme caution and to return any fire."

Moving with that extreme caution and deliberation toward Xom Lang, the thirty-odd men of Calley's first platoon expected at any moment to come under the intense fire they had been warned they would receive. They were tense, as though girding themselves to repel the bullets which would hit them. But there was only silence from Xom Lang.

As they approached the first houses, they broke into smaller units—squads and even smaller, just a few men separating and advancing on different targets. And from that moment on, no man saw all the action, saw all that happened. Each man's knowledge of the events of the next few hours that morning—as was the knowledge of those inside the settlement waiting for the Americans to arrive—was limited by his own immediate area of combat and vision, to his own particular ground inside and around Xom Lang and nearby Binh Dong. The events of those next hours, and particularly that next forty minutes, then, were necessarily episodic and chaotic; there was no order, no sequence, merely action and reaction, here and there and everywhere.

Any attempt, then, to describe what happened—on the basis of the recollections of the American soldiers as related to this reporter and others, and of Vietnamese reliving the carnage in conversations with me—can only, at best, attempt to reveal the chaos of the whole and the separateness of the small individual scenes.

With Sergeant Mitchell in the lead, five men of Charley Company descended from their chopper right outside the hamlet. They began moving toward the houses in a single line, Mitchell in the lead. Paul Meadlo remembers that "there was one man, a gook in a shelter, all huddled down in there, and the soldier called out and said there's a gook over here." Sergeant Mitchell brusquely gave the orders to shoot. "And so then the man was shot. So we moved on into the village."

"When the attack started," Sergeant Charles West recalls, "it couldn't have been stopped by anyone. We were mad and we had been told that the enemy was there and we were going in there to give them a fight for what they had done to our dead buddies."

Approaching Xom Lang, "we went in shooting," West says. "We'd shoot into the hootches and there were people running around. There were big craters in the village from the bombing. When I got there I saw some of the people, some of the women and kids all torn up."

"I was just coming to the first row of houses, with five or six other guys," says another member of the platoon, "when we heard this noise behind us. Everybody was scared and on edge, and keyed up, too, to kill, and somebody turned quick and snapped off a shot. We all turned and shot. And there was this big old water buffalo, I guess that's what it was, standing in the middle of this field behind us. Everybody was shooting at it and you could see little puffs jumping out where the bullets hit. It was like something in slow motion, and finally that cow just slumped down and collapsed." His face contorted by the remembrance, he adds, "Now it seems kind of funny, but it didn't then. And once the shooting started, I guess it affected everyone. From then on it was like nobody could stop. Everyone was just shooting at everything and anything, like the ammo wouldn't ever give out."

The contagion of slaughter was spreading throughout the platoon.

Combat photographer Ronald Haeberle and Army Correspondent Jay Roberts had requested permission to accompany a combat mission in order to get both pictures and a story of American soldiers in action. They had been assigned to Charley Company and to Calley's platoon. Leaving their helicopter with about ten or fifteen other soldiers, they came upon a cow being slaughtered, and then the picture turned sickenly grisly. "Off to the right," Haeberle said, "a woman's form, a head appeared from some brush. All the other GI's started firing at her, aiming at her, firing at her over and over again."

The bullets riddled the woman's body. She slumped against a well pump in the middle of the rice paddy, her head caught between two of its poles. She was obviously already dead, but the infection, the hysteria was now ascendant. The men were oblivious to everything but slaughter. "They just kept shooting at her. You could see the bones flying in the air, chip by chip."

There were the sounds: the shots running into and over each other from inside the hamlet; it sounded as though everyone had his rifle on automatic, no one bothering to save ammunition by switching to single shot. And not drowned by the sharp bark of the rifles and duller thuds of grenades were screams; they sounded like women and children, but how can anyone tell in that kind of moment from a distance who is screaming?

Four or five Americans were outside the hamlet, moving along its perimeter. The job of their platoon was to seal it off and so prevent the VC inside from fleeing from Calley's men, to catch them in a pincer and slaughter them. Vernardo Simpson and these other soldiers were probing the bushes on the outskirts, delicately, searching for mines and booby traps. As they neared the first group of houses, a man dressed in black pajamas —the dress convinced Simpson that he must be a VC even though black pajamas were traditional peasant dress—suddenly appeared from nowhere, from some bushes and began running toward the hamlet. A woman and child popped up from the same underbrush and started "running away from us toward some huts."

"Dong lai! Dong lai!" The Americans shouted after the Vietnamese. But they kept on running. Lieutenant Brooks, the leader of this second platoon, gave the orders to shoot. If these people did not stop on command, then they must necessarily be

VC. "This is what I did," Simpson says. "I shot them, the lady and the little boy. He was about two years old."

A woman and a child? Why?

"I was reluctant, but I was following a direct order. If I didn't do this I could stand court martial for not following a direct order."

Before the day was over, Simpson says, he would have killed at least ten Vietnamese in Xom Lang.

With the number killed there, his total was about the average for each soldier.

When the shelling stopped, Pham Phon crept from the bunker near his hootch. About fifty meters away, he saw a small group of American soldiers. Poking his head back into the bunker, he told his wife and three children—two sons aged nine and four, and a seven year old daughter—to come up and walk slowly toward the Americans.

Like almost all Vietnamese in the hamlets around the country, Phon and his family had learned from the three previous American visits and from the tales told by refugees who had come to Xom Lang to seek shelter after their hamlets had been turned into battlegrounds and from tales carried by others from far away, just how to act when American troops arrived.

It was imperative not to run, either toward the Americans or away from them. If you ran, the Americans would think that you were VC, running away from them or running toward them with a grenade, and they would shoot.

It was imperative not to stay inside the house or the bunker. If you did, then the Americans would think you were VC hiding in ambush, and they would shoot or throw grenades into the house or bunker.

It was imperative to walk slowly toward the Americans, with hands in plain view, or to gather in small groups in some central spot and wait for the Americans to arrive—but never to gather in large groups, for then the Americans would think the group was VC waiting to fire. It was absolutely imperative to show only servility so that the Americans would know that you were not VC and had only peaceful intent.

So Phon and his family walked slowly toward the soldiers. The three children smiled and shouted, "Hello! Hello! Okay! Okay!"

Only this time, unlike the three previous American visitations, there were no answering grins, no gifts of candy and rations. The Americans pointed their rifles at the family and sternly ordered them to walk to the canal about a hundred meters away.

Inside the hamlet, the men of the first platoon were racing from house to house. They planted dynamite and explosive to the brick ones and blew them into dust. They set fires with their lighters to the thatched roofs and to the hootches, watched them flare into a ritual bonfire and then raced on to the next hootch. Some soldiers were pulling people from bunkers and out of the houses and herding them into groups. Some of the Vietnamese tried to run and were immediately shot. Others didn't seem to know what was happening, didn't understand what the Americans were doing or why. But most of them behaved as they had learned they must behave. Meekly they followed any order given.

Some of the groups were marched away in the direction of the canal, and those who straggled behind, could not keep up, were promptly shot.

There were soldiers standing outside the hootches, watching them burn, and as Vietnamese suddenly emerged from the pyres, would shoot them.

And through everything, through the sound of gunfire and through the crackling of flames, through the smoke that had begun to cover everything like a pall, came high pitched screams of pain and terror, bewildered cries, pleading cries. All were ignored.

Michael Bernhardt remembers coming into the hamlet and seeing his fellow soldiers "doing a whole lot of shooting up. But none of it was incoming. I'd been around enough to tell that. I figured we were advancing on the village with fire power."

Inside the hamlet, Bernhardt "saw these guys doing strange things. They were doing it in three ways. They were setting fire to the hootches and huts and waiting for the people to come out and then shooting them. They were going into the hootches and shooting them up. They were gathering people in groups and shooting them."

The raging fever in the other members of his platoon stunned and shocked Bernhardt. He watched one soldier shooting at everything he saw, blazing away indiscriminately and laughing hysterically as he kept pulling the trigger, kept his finger on the trigger until all the bullets in a clip were gone, then throwing away the clip and reloading and starting again. And laughing all the time. "He just couldn't stop. He thought it was funny, funny, funny."

Bernhardt says that he was sickened and appalled by what he was seeing, yet he felt helpless to do anything about it, helpless to do anything but stand and watch. "I found out," he told one reporter, "that an act like that, you know, murder for no reason, that could be done by just about anybody."

All through that bloody hour, Bernhardt kept his rifle in its sling, pointing toward the ground. He felt he had no reason to unsling it, no reason to aim it at anybody.

For Private Herbert Carter it was too much, a nightmare from which there seemed no awakening. "People began coming out of their hootches and the guys shot them and burned the hootches—or burned the hootches and then shot the people when they came out. Sometimes they would round up a bunch and shoot them together. It went on like that for what seemed like all day. Some of the guys seemed to be having a lot of fun. They were wisecracking and yelling, 'Chalk that one up for me.' "

When he could stand the sight no longer, Carter turned and stumbled out of the hamlet. He sat down under a tree and shot himself in the foot.

He was Charley Company's only casualty that morning.

When the first shells hurled their way into Xom Lang, Nguyen Thi Nien and her family took shelter in their bunker adjacent to their house. In the bunker with her were her eighty-year-old father-in-law, her sister and her sister's seven-year-old daughter, her own husband and their three children. They cowered in the bunker for a considerable length of time. Finally they heard steady rifle fire around them and American voices yelling: "VC di ra! VC di ra!"—VC, get out! VC, get out!

The family crawled slowly and carefully out of the bunker, making every effort to display no hostility. But once they were out they noticed that the Americans were still some distance away. Taking her youngest child, still a baby, in one arm and holding her second youngest by the hand, Nguyen Thi Nien started away, toward the rice paddies. She did not run, but walked on steadily. Her husband and the oldest child started to follow her. But her sister and her sister's daughter hung back, then started in another direction. And her father-in-law turned and started back to the house.

"I am too old," she remembers him calling after her. "I can not keep up. You get out and I will stay here to keep the house."

There was almost no argument. "We told him," Nguyen Thi Nien says, "all right, you are too old. So you stay here and if the GI's arrive you ask them not to shoot you and not to burn the house."

The old man called that that was exactly what he intended to do. He would stand guard over the family home. But then Nguyen Thi Nien's husband decided that he could not leave his father alone in the house. He turned, sending the oldest child after his wife and the other children, and went back to his father. They stood outside the house for a brief moment arguing. The son trying to convince the old man to get out of the house and go with them to the paddies before the Americans arrived. The Americans were approaching and they could hear the clatter of shots, they could see the flames licking around other houses, and the smoke.

But the old man remained adamant. He was too old, he kept insisting. He could not make it to the paddy. He refused to leave, turning from his son and starting into the house.

The Americans were almost on them; the firing was all around them now. Nien realized that he could wait no longer. If he were to escape the approaching Americans—he realized by then that this was not a friendly visit, that the Americans were hostile this time and were shooting at everything—he would have to flee immediately.

About four hundred meters away, he saw his wife and three children just ducking into the rice paddies, safe. He started after them. Ahead of him, just a few feet, was an old woman, a nearby neighbor. "But suddenly," he says, "five GI's were in front of me, about a hundred meters or so from me. The GI's saw us and started to shoot and the lady was killed. I was hit and so I lay down. Then I saw blood coming from my stomach and so I took a handkerchief and put it over my wound. I lay on the ground there for a little while and then I tried to get back to my house, to my old father and my sister-in-law and her child who must still be there. I could not walk very well and so I was crawling. On the way back to my house I saw five children and one father lying dead on the ground. When I reached my house, I saw it was on fire. Through the fire I could see the bodies of my old father, my sister-in-law and her child inside the house. Then I lost consciousness and I do not know anything more of what happened."

All around there was burning and explosions, shooting and the dead, the screams of the living and, beginning, the sweet smell of burning flesh in the hootches turned into funeral pyres. And, now and again, there was the awful hysterical laughter of one soldier or another. Some of the American faces had expressions which frightened and shocked their friends, those friends at least who emerged from the mass hysteria, which seemed to fill the entire company, long enough to look around them.

"I was just coming into the middle of that ville," remembers one soldier, refusing to look around or to meet his questioner's eyes as he talks, "and I saw this guy. He was one of my best friends in the company. But honest to Christ, at first I didn't even recognize him. He was kneeling on the ground, this absolutely incredible . . . I don't know what you'd call it, a smile or a snarl or something, but anyway, his whole face was distorted. He was covered with smoke, his face streaked with it, and it looked like there was blood on him, too. You couldn't tell, but there was blood everywhere. Anyway, he was kneeling there holding this grenade launcher, and he was launching grenades at the hootches. A couple of times he launched grenades at groups of people. The grenades would explode, you know, KAPLOW, and then you'd see pieces of bodies flying around. Some of the groups were just piles of bodies. But I remember there was this one group a little distance away. Maybe there was ten people, most of them women and little kids, huddled all together and you could see they were really scared, they just couldn't seem to move. Anyway, he turns around toward them and lets fly with a grenade. It landed right in the middle of them. You could hear the screams and then the sound and then see the pieces of bodies scatter out, and the whole area just suddenly turned red like somebody had turned on a faucet."

Did you do anything to try to stop him?

"You got rocks or something? All you had to do was take one look at him, at his face and you knew the best thing was to leave him alone. I think if I had even said a word to him at all, he would have turned and killed me and not thought a damn thing about it."

The artillery and bombs had stopped. The noise of the choppers had faded away only to be replaced by the rattle of small arms. Ngo Ngo Thininh huddled in fear in the bunker outside Mr. Sam's house with the other members of her family, waiting. Then she heard the sound of boots outside overhead, near the bunker. Softly, Mr. Sam ordered the members of the family to emerge. After all, these were the Americans. His son was fighting for the ARVN and he was known to support the government, to oppose the VC. Hadn't he been taken to a VC prison? So he feared nothing. The Americans were friends.

But Ngo Ngo Thininh was still terrified. She waited while the men, the older women and the children clambered out to greet the Americans. As she heard them moving off, away from the bunker and the house, she darted up from underground and without pausing to look around dashed as fast as she could away from the hamlet into the rice paddies, crouching there and hiding for a little while. Then, as the noise in the village seemed to die down, she crept through the paddies and made her way slowly to safety in the next village to the west.

Why did you run from the Americans? You didn't know at the time that this wasn't just another patrol coming through, did you?

"No."

Then why did you run?

"I was not pregnant at that time."

I'm not sure I understand what you mean.

"I am only a woman and so I feared GI's. Therefore, I must escape the house, escape the area."

Why?

"Because my husband tells me that if GI's come to the area, I must run, escape. Otherwise, if I am not pregnant, they will do things to me."

You believe this?

"All the young girls, all the women have heard that it is so."

And your husband told you this, too?

"Yes, my husband tells me this."

Was he with the VC?

"No. He is ARVN soldier."

There is a well-documented theory of many psychiatrists that sex and violence are two aspects of the same emotion. And that sometimes violence will set loose uncontrollable erotic desires. It has happened often enough in civilized society during peacetime: the incidence of well-publicized sex murders is too well-known to even bother to comment on. If violence during peace can let loose erotic behavior, violence during war seems often to make such desires even less controllable. There had been evidence of this on patrols before. And there was evidence of it again in Xom Lang. The killing, the indiscriminate slaughter all around brought such emotions to the surface in some of the men in the platoon.

Jay Roberts and Ronald Haeberle moved about the havoc taking pictures. They came upon one group of Americans surrounding a small group of women, children and a teen-age girl. She was perhaps twelve or thirteen and was wearing the traditional peasant black pajamas. One of the Americans grabbed her by the shoulders while another began to try to strip the pajamas off her, pulling at the top of the blouse to undo it.

"Let's see what she's made of," one of the soldiers laughed.

Another moved close to her, laughing and pointing at her. "VC, boom-boom," he said. He was telling her in the GI patois that she was a whore for the VC, and indicating that if she did it for them why not for the Americans.

A third soldier examined her carefully and then turned to the others. "Jesus," he said, "I'm horny."

All around there were burning buildings and bodies and the sounds of firing and screams. But the Americans seemed totally oblivious to anything but the girl. They had almost stripped her when her mother rushed over and tried to help her escape. She clutched at the American soldiers, scratched them, clawed at their faces, screaming invectives at them. They pushed her off. One soldier slapped her across the face; another hit her in the stomach with his fist; a third kicked her in the behind, knocking her sprawling to the ground.

But the mother's actions had given the girl a chance to escape a little. She took shelter behind some of the other women in the group and tried to button the top of her blouse. Haeberle stepped in, knelt and took a picture of the scene.

Roberts remembers that at that moment, "when they noticed Ron, they left off and turned away as if everything was normal. Then a soldier asked, 'Well, what'll we do with 'em?'

" 'Kill 'em,' another answered.

"I heard an M-60 go off, a light machine gun, and when we turned all of them and the kids with them were dead."

Somewhere else in the hamlet another soldier says that he saw a buddy suddenly pull a small child out of a group of women. "She was just a little thing," he says. "She couldn't have been more than five or six."

What happened?

"He dragged her into one of these brick houses that hadn't been blown up yet."

And?

"I don't know. I didn't go inside with him. And I don't like to talk about it." He pauses for a few moments, looking away, and then he speaks in a muffled voice, toward the table. "He was in there maybe five, ten minutes. Then he comes out, turns around and throws a grenade into the house."

Another soldier says he saw a teen-age girl running across a rice paddy, trying to hide from an American who was chasing her. As he watched, he saw this American soldier aim with his rifle and shoot. The girl gave a cry and fell down. The soldier went after her and vanished into the paddy. A few minutes later there was another shot from the area and then the soldier walked back from the field into the hamlet.

Nguyen Thi Doc is over seventy, an ancient, stooped peasant woman with a stoic, expressionless face. Today she squats in misery in the doorway of the hootch she shares with a small grandson and a small granddaughter in the refugee camp across from Xom Lang.

On that March morning she was just beginning to make breakfast for her husband, her son, two daughters and nine grandchildren from three to sixteen. They were all gathered around her waiting for their rice. When the bombardment started, all took shelter in the bunker just outside the door. When the shells ceased, they emerged and went back into the house to eat.

A few minutes later Nguyen Thi Doc "heard the Americans come down from the sky." Within minutes they were at her doorway. Without saying a word, they began spraying the inside of the house with machine gun fire. Her husband, her son, her two daughters and seven of her grandchildren—the oldest seven—were killed immediately. Nguyen Thi Doc was shot in the arm; her five year old granddaughter was shot in the foot. Today it is scarred and shriveled and the child limps through the camp, often hiding from others. Only the youngest child, a little boy, escaped unharmed.

The Americans then set fire to the house. Somehow, Nguyen Thi Doc managed to get outside, taking her granddaughter and grandson with her, and from the yard they watched the house burn, inside of it the rest of her family.

Now she sits in the refugee camp, asking no questions why it happened. "I am too old," she says. "I have no idea why the GI's come and do this thing. The thing I must do is to make money to take care of these children. They have no one else. And I am too old. I just want to die."

Just outside the village there was a big pile of bodies. Jay Roberts sees this "really tiny kid—he only had a shirt on—nothing else. He came over to the people and held the hand of one of the dead. One of the GI's behind me dropped into a kneeling position thirty meters from this kid and killed him with a single shot."

Haeberle sees two small children, maybe four or five years old. "A guy with an M-16 fired at the first boy and the older boy fell over him to protect the smaller one. Then they fired six more shots. It was done very businesslike."

A small boy, three or four, suddenly appears from nowhere on the trail in front of a group of Americans. He is wounded in the arm. Michael Terry sees "the boy clutching his wounded arm with his other hand while the blood trickled between his fingers. He was staring around himself in shock and disbelief at what he saw. He just stood there with big eyes staring around like he didn't understand what was happening. Then the captain's radio operator put a burst of 16 into him."

When Paul Meadlo came into Xom Lang, Lieutenant Calley set him and some of the other men to work gathering the people together in groups in a central location. "There was about forty, forty-five people that we gathered in the center of the village,"

Meadlo told an interviewer. "And we placed them in there, and it was like a little island, right there in the center of the village."

The soldiers forced the people in the group to squat on the ground. "Lieutenant Calley came over and said, 'You know what to do with them, don't you?' And I said, 'Yes.' So I took it for granted he just wanted us to watch them. And he left and came back about ten or fifteen minutes later, and said, 'How come you ain't killed them yet?' And I told him that I didn't think he wanted us to kill them, that you just wanted us to guard them. He said, 'No, I want them dead.'"

At first Meadlo was surprised by the order—not shocked or horrified, but surprised. "But three, four guys heard it and then he stepped back about ten, fifteen feet, and he started shooting them. And he told me to start shooting. I poured about four clips into the group."

A clip is seventeen rounds. Meadlo fired sixty-eight rounds into this group of people. "I fired them on automatic," he said, "so you can't . . . you just spray the area on them and so you can't know how many you killed 'cause they were going fast. So I might have killed ten or fifteen of them."

One slaughter was over, but there was more to come, and the thirst for blood had become so contagious that no one thought anything about what he was doing. "We started to gather them up, more people," Meadlo says, "and we had about seven or eight people that we was gonna put into a hootch and we dropped a hand grenade in there with them."

Then Meadlo and several other soldiers took a group of civilians—almost exclusively women and children, some of the children still too young to walk—toward one of the two canals on the outskirts of Xom Lang. "They had about seventy, seventy-five people all gathered up. So we threw ours in with them and Lieutenant Calley told me, he said, 'Meadlo, we got another job to do.' And so he walked over to the people and started pushing them off and started shooting."

Taking his cue from Calley, Meadlo and then the other members of this squad "started pushing them off and we started shooting them. So altogether we just pushed them all off and just started using automatics on them. And somebody told us to switch off to single shot so that we could save ammo. So we switched off to single shot and shot a few more rounds."

And all the time the Vietnamese at the canal were screaming and pleading with the Americans for mercy.

Led by a group of GI's, Pham Phon, his wife and three small children reached the canal. There, "I saw a lot of people who were grouping there, people were crying, especially babies were crying. But GI's stand on both sides of the canal so nobody . . . both banks of the canal, so nobody can move away."

For a time, the Americans kept the Vietnamese standing along side the canal. But soon, to make sure that none tried to escape, they forced the people to sit down. Meanwhile, says Phon, "another group of GI's search the next hamlet, the sub-hamlet called Binh Dong, about five hundred meters from my hamlet. And the GI's had other people from this new hamlet. They brought them to the canal. There must have been more than one hundred, but who can count at such a time."

When Phon saw the Americans herding this large group from Binh Dong to the canal, he had a premonition of disaster. And this was re-inforced by the sounds of gunfire that he heard from Xom Lang. "I tell my wife and my kids, slip into the canal when GI not looking. We watch for our chance and we do that. So then the GI begin to shoot at the standing people and at the sitting people on the banks of the canal. They fall into the canal and cover us with their bodies. So we were not wounded, myself, my wife and my two sons. My little daughter, only seven years old, she was wounded in the arm when GI's shoot into the canal when they heard the people groaning and making much noise."

Was this just a large group of GI's, acting on their own without any kind of direction, without any leader?

"No. There was a leader."

Did you notice who he was?

"One man. He waved his hand and GI's started to shoot."

Could you tell whether he was an officer or not?

"I could not tell. I do not know different GI's. All Americans look the same, except some are black and some are white, but that is the only difference."

Well, was this a white man or a black man?

"A white man."

Was he a tall man or a small man?

"He was a small man, small like a Vietnamese. He waved his hand like that and then he shoot his gun and then all GI's shoot their guns."

Just as the slaughter at the canal began, Michael Terry happened to be passing by. "They had them in a group, standing over a ditch—just like a Nazi-type thing," he remembers. "One officer ordered a kid to machine gun everybody down. But the kid couldn't do it. He threw the machine gun down and the officer picked it up. I don't remember seeing any men in the ditch. Mostly woman and kids."

Terry left for another part of the hamlet. Later he returned. Calley and his men had left by then and only a small group had stayed behind. Terry was at the canal, sitting on a mound eating some chow with William Doherty. As they were eating, the two noticed that "some of them were still breathing. They were pretty badly shot up. They weren't going to get any medical help, and so we shot them, shot maybe five of them."

In another part of Xom Lang, James Bergthold was moving just behind another soldier carrying a light machine gun. This soldier was moving from house to house, spraying in through the doors, not even looking where he was shooting. He came to one hootch, opened up and then strolled away. Bergthold stopped and looked in. An old man was writhing on the floor in pain, screaming, with large pieces of his legs shot away. Bergthold took his rifle and shot the old man. "Just to put him out of his misery."

All through Xom Lang and around it, the slaughter and the destruction continued endlessly, senselessly. Houses were blown apart and burned. Dead bodies were tossed into the pyres which had once been their homes, or they were left where they had fallen. Animals were slaughtered. Haeberle remembers one scene of a GI stabbing a cow over and over again with his bayonet while the blood spurted in all directions and other soldiers stood around watching and laughing and commenting on his technique. Dead animals and dead bodies were thrown down wells to pollute the water supply. And everywhere, it seemed, was Lieutenant Calley.

But for some Americans, at least, there was no joy in what was happening in Xom Lang, no glory and no victory. Haeberle saw one GI go over to a little boy who had been badly torn apart by a fusillade and with infinite tenderness cover him with a blanket.

And that night, when Nguyen Chi returned to the hamlet to seek her family, she found her three young sons still alive. When the first shells had fallen, the boys had taken their buffalo from the barn into the fields to hide it. At one point they raised their heads to see what was happening. Near them was an American soldier. He stared at them for a moment, then with great urgency motioned for them to duck again. No one is certain who this American was, but he may have been Pvt. Olson—like Bernhardt, he refused to shoot anyone that morning.

This chaotic dance of death was not enacted before an empty

auditorium. There were spectators, an audience viewing the drama like ancient Romans at the martyrdom of the Christians. These spectators had a panoramic view.

There were the helicopters circling back and forth, hovering over Xom Lang, reconnoitering the area for signs of the VC and for information on what was going on below. The pilot of one of these choppers was Warrant Officer Hugh C. Thompson of Decatur, Georgia.

The gunner in this helicopter, Specialist Fourth Class Larry Colburn, says that as they were hovering low over one part of the hamlet, they "noticed people dead and wounded along the road and all through the village. There was an irrigation ditch full of bodies. We noticed that some people were still alive. We didn't know what had happened."

Thompson decided to drop down and evacuate some of the wounded. But the helicopter was already pretty full with his own crew, and so he radioed for the gunships to return and help lift the wounded civilians, mainly children, to safety. Then he spotted a group of about fifteen or a dozen children in the midst of the dead and the dying. "We went down," Colburn says, "and our crew chief brought out a little boy about two years old. He seemed in shock."

Huddled in a bunker a short distance away were about a dozen more children. Once again Thompson's radio operator called for the gunships to come in and help the children, ferry them to the nearest field hospital. As Thompson's helicopter lifted off, Colburn noticed that "there must have been about seventy-five or eighty people in a ditch—some dead, some wounded. I had never seen so many people dead in one place before."

The chopper took off and ferried the children to the hospital, then returned to Xom Lang. Thompson spotted more children caught in a bunker in the midst of firing. He set his helicopter

138

down again to try to rescue the children. This time he got out himself and started toward one small child by himself. Nearby he spotted Calley moving toward the child. Thompson motioned for Calley to come toward him.

Calley approached Thompson and those in the vicinity could see signs of a bitter argument though the noise of the helicopter engines and the gunfire drowned out the words. Thompson started toward the child again. Calley made a motion with his rifle. Thompson, blazing with rage, turned abruptly and strode across to the helicopter. There he told one of his waist gunners to aim his machine gun "at that officer," and if the officer attempted to intervene again, to shoot him. Thompson then went back, picked up the child and carried him back to the chopper and took off once again.

With the chopper and the child gone, Calley walked across to his radio operator, Charles Sledge. Calley said, "That guy isn't very happy with the way we're running this operation. But I don't care. He's not in charge."

Almost incredibly, nearly nineteen months later, on October 15, 1969, Hugh Thompson was awarded the Distinguished Flying Cross for his act of courage that morning. The Army, however, was theoretically not aware at the moment of just what that bravery had entailed in Son My village, in the hamlet of Tu Cung, in the sub-hamlet of Xom Lang.

The citation read in part:

". . . . Warrant Officer Thompson's aircraft was performing a reconnaissance and screening mission for friendly forces near Quang Ngai. After spotting approximately fifteen young children who were trying to hide in a bunker between Viet Cong positions and advancing friendly forces, Warrant Officer Thompson landed his helicopter near the children and moved them to a secure area.

". . . later, he located a wounded Vietnamese child, caught

in the intense crossfire. Disregarding his own safety, he again landed his own helicopter and evacuated the wounded child to the Quang Ngai hospital.

"Warrant Officer Thompson's heroic actions saved several innocent lives, while his sound judgement greatly enhanced Vietnamese-American relations in the operational area."

It had indeed been a heroic action on the part of Thompson. But the only danger he faced was not from the VC, for there were no VC fighting in that area. The only danger he faced was from American troops who had run wild.

And where, all this time, was the leader whose men were turning Xom Lang into a charnel house?

He was, he says, outside the hamlet, in his command post and moving about the perimeter, linked with his three platoons—Calley's first inside Xom Lang, Brooks' second, on the north, and third platoon of La Cross held in reserve to the west—by field radio. Captain Ernest Medina says that only once did he enter the hamlet, and that was to meet troops coming through from the other side. "I wasn't looking for anything in particular. They were burning the village. They were shooting the livestock and closing the wells." He saw, he says, about twenty-five civilian bodies and he thought that they had been killed "by artillery fire from the gunships or small arms fire. I did not ask how the people had been killed and I did not go over to inspect the individual bodies."

Knowing how Medina had acted—or, rather, not acted—toward Vietnamese since arriving in country, it would not be at all surprising that he did not ask how they had been killed or even care very much.

Most of the time, according to Medina, he was moving back and forth, checking out reports from the helicopter spotters and trying to keep in constant touch with his platoons.

At one point, according to Medina's own account, he received a report from a helicopter hovering a short distance away that there were dead VC in a rice paddy near the hamlet. The chopper dropped smoke bombs to mark the spot. In response to urgings from Major Charles Calhoun, a superior officer of the brigade who was monitoring reports at LZ Dottie, Medina sent Brooks' platoon in that direction, leaving Calley and his men alone within Xom Lang.

Later another helicopter reported more dead VC with weapons to the south of the hamlet. Medina says that he decided to check this report out himself since all his men seemed to be otherwise engaged. With his command group, he started walking toward the spot which had been marked by smoke bombs. A chopper hovered overhead. The command group had walked only a short distance when it came upon the bodies of a man, woman and small child literally ripped apart. A little further on, near the smoke-marked site, Medina saw a woman in black pajamas sprawled on the ground. He thought that she, like the others they had passed, was dead and he started past her. Then out of the corner of his eye he saw her move.

"As I turned," Medina says, "I thought to myself, 'You're dead, you fool.'" He raised his rifle as fast as he could and snapped off a shot, hitting and killing the woman. He noticed at once that there was no weapon near her. "I didn't feel very good about it and left."

This, Medina maintains firmly, was the only killing he personally had a hand in that day.

But both his story of the sole killing and his claim that it was the only one he did that morning have been disputed by the men under his command.

Michael Bernhardt says that he was with Medina when the woman was killed. As Bernhardt tells it, they were walking along when they saw a woman pretending to pick rice. "She was about a hundred meters away. She had a basket in her hand.

Maybe Medina thought she had a grenade in the basket, but she would had to have a fantastic arm to throw it that far. Medina lifted his rifle to his shoulder, looked down the barrel and pulled the trigger."

The woman dropped. They approached closer. Bernhardt says that Medina "got up real close, about three or six feet and shot at her a couple of times and finished her off."

And Richard Pendleton has accused Medina of another killing that morning. According to Pendleton, he was with the captain when the slaughter at Xom Lang had just about run its race. "But some guys were still shooting people who were running around the village. There were big groups of bodies lying on the ground in gullies and paddies." Among a group of perhaps fifteen dead adults, Pendleton saw a little boy standing, searching among the bodies. "I guess the boy's mother was one of them." The group stopped for a moment, "and I looked over and saw Medina shoot him. I don't know why he did it except that there was a bunch of bodies there."

In the heat and the passion of that morning, it is almost impossible to know who is telling the real truth about any of the events or any of the people, or if there is even any real truth. And perhaps it is less than the major quest in the story of what happened and why it happened that morning in March to discover and decide just who killed whom, where and when. Many hundreds of people, most of them children, women and old men, were slaughtered at Xom Lang and Binh Dong. A mass hysteria swept over a large number of American soldiers who became executioners, indiscriminate butchers. And in the horror of it all, is there really sense and meaning in saying that one did such and such and this one did this and that? In a senseless slaughter, the attempt to fix blame for specific killings on specific people is an attempt to find sense and logic where it does not and cannot exist. The responsibility for what happened at Xom Lang lies not just with the man or the men who pulled the triggers and threw the grenades. The responsibility goes further and higher.

Eventually slaughter, even a slaughter caused by mass psychosis, must end. Either there are no more alive to serve as sacrificial victims or some higher power intervenes. At Xom Lang, it was intervention from above that brought the killing to an end.

In the air overhead, the choppers had been whirling back and forth since the firing began. There had been a constant communications hum between Medina and the helicopters, Medina and the home base at LZ Dottie, and Medina and his platoons. After the firing had lasted for some little time, Medina got a radio call from one of the choppers. Pendleton who was standing near him says that the captain blanched and then began "running about yelling to stop the shooting the choppers had seen. Until then, he didn't do anything."

Specialist Fifth Class John Kinch remembers that, with Medina in the lead, a group of soldiers was moving into the hamlet, with bodies piled thick around them. "Colonel Barker, the task force commander, was overhead in his helicopter," Kinch says. "He came through over the radio saying he had got word from the medevac chopper that there were bodies lying everywhere and what was going on. I heard Captain Medina tell him, 'I don't know what they are doing. The first platoon's in the lead. I am trying to stop it.' Just after that he called the first platoon and said, 'That's enough shooting for today.' Colonel Barker called down again for a body count and Medina got back on the horn and said, 'I have a body count of three hundred ten.' "

And so the battle for Xom Lang—what the men in Charley Company that morning, as they were approaching it, had thought was the VC stronghold called My Lai or "Pinkville"

143

and which was marked on their maps as My Lai (4)—came to an end. To many of those who were there, it seemed that the time had been endless, that it had begun and gone on and on and on. But it had all taken less than an hour.

And in this supposed stronghold of the communist guerrillas, the U.S. troops found exactly three rifles, which Bernhardt says were American, some ammunition and a couple of grenades.

No one can ever be exactly certain just how many Vietnamese died at Xom Lang, or Thuan Yen—the Place Where Trouble Does Not Come—and Binh Dong. Many of those who were killed were burned in the hootches; many were blown apart; there were whole families exterminated so that there were no survivors to claim the dead; and in the hamlet lived a number of refugees from other villages and hamlets who were not considered by the people to be really a part of their own.

But enough survivors make the same estimate to set the figure at somewhere over four hundred, perhaps as many as four hundred and thirty. Of these dead, according to several survivors, about two hundred and ninety were natives of Xom Lang; forty more were refugees, Vietnamese who had sought shelter in what they considered a peaceful hamlet after they had been driven from their own embattled ones; and another hundred dead were from the adjoining sub-hamlet of Binh Dong. Some of these were killed in Binh Dong and more were marched to the canal to join their Xom Lang neighbors in front of a firing squad.

By nine o'clock that morning Charley Company began moving out of Xom Lang. Some men remained behind in the hamlet to finish the burning and destruction. The rest began moving east to meet eventually with Bravo Company which had been set down near the coast to the southeast with orders to "search-and-destroy" and move inland, linking up with Charley Company for a joint night bivouac.

But if the killing was over in Xom Lang, it was not finished elsewhere in Son My village. In fact, as the shooting stopped at Xom Lang, it was about to begin near the coast.

For as Charley Company was beginning its movement from Xom Lang, about two miles away, to the southeast just inland from the sea, in the sub-hamlet of My Hoi—marked on the American military maps as My Khe (4)—a part of Co Luy hamlet, there was more action and more dead.

The army was later to report—in a summary initially just as ignored as the original reports of the assault on Xom Lang, or My Lai (4), and ignored for much longer—that a platoon under the command of Lieutenant Thomas Willingham of Bravo Company had run into enemy fire when it was airlifted into the area near the beach. According to this army release, the platoon killed thirty Vietnamese enemy and then killed eight more in "an enemy underground complex."

My Hoi is divided into two sections, separated by the Kinh Giang River, a shallow stream that flows along the coast from the Cho Mai River in the north to the Tra Khuc River in the south, turning much of Co Luy hamlet effectively into an island joined to the rest of the hamlet and to Son My village by narrow bridges and shallow fords. At My Hoi, the Kinh Giang is about thirty meters wide, though shallow enough most of the year for residents to wade back and forth across it. About half the sub-hamlet lies on either side of the river.

Nguyen Van Danh's house was on the seaside. All morning, he and the other people in the hamlet had been listening to the intense fire coming from the west, in the direction of Tu Cung hamlet, concerned about what was happening but afraid to move in that direction to find out.

Just before nine in the morning, however, some helicopters suddenly appeared over My Hoi. As the people stared up at them, shells began to rain down into the hamlet and little puffs of dust began to run through the main street as machine gun fire strafed the area.

"When we heard the cannon shell fall into the hamlet," Danh says, "we went into the bunkers to take shelter." The shelling stopped after about fifteen minutes and the people in the bunkers looked out. They could see more helicopters beginning to set down. The choppers landed across the Kinh Giang at the edge of the western half of My Hoi. Most of the people in the east ducked back into their bunkers and remained hidden.

"We heard lots of shots," Danh, the deputy sub-hamlet chief, remembers, "from rifles and machine guns. But we stayed in the bunkers, looking out only sometimes and seeing the GI's operating in the other part of My Hoi, across the river. They did not come to my part, just stayed there on the other side of the water."

The shooting, the burning and the detonations from grenades and explosives lasted for more than an hour, according to Danh and others from the sub-hamlet now sheltered in refugee camps. And amid the firing, they could hear screams and cries.

When at last the shooting died down to a sporadic shot now and again, those still safe on the eastern shore of the river looked again from their bunkers. The Americans were still in the western section of My Hoi, burning and blasting the houses, killing the livestock. No Vietnamese could be seen. The Americans remained at their work until nearly one in the afternoon, and then they moved out, heading inland. "When the GI's left, we . . . some of the people and I . . . we went across the river to see what had happened. The houses were all burning and blown up and there were lots of people killed. Lots of families had four, five, six, seven, eight people killed. There were lots of families had four or five people killed. In my family across the river I had three nephews—four, six and seven years old—killed. There were ninety-seven, a hundred people killed in that part of my hamlet."

Those standing around Danh, listening attentively, nod with agreement, and one man says, "There were more. I know there were more." But most of the others seem satisfied with Danh's estimate.

Then Danh adds, "If the massacre did not happen on that day but the next day or the one after that, then many more people would be killed."

Why?

"Because the people had just begun to come home to the hamlet from the camps. I myself and about one hundred others had just returned the day before. There were more, maybe more than a hundred others that I knew were coming back in the next days. So if the killings had happened one day, two days later, then the killings would be more."

But isn't it true that there were a lot of VC in the hamlet?

"At first, yes, but not lately. And the government had told us that the hamlet was safe. That is why we returned from the camps. Most of the VC were in My Khe, one klick north of my hamlet."

My Khe is what is marked on the American military maps as My Lai (1) in My Lai hamlet and is colored in pink.

And then Danh says, "This is the first time the GI's arrived in my hamlet. Before it had always been the ARVN. I wonder why the GI's kill the young kids. But I am alive and I must take care of my kids, those who are still alive. So I must not wonder about this too much."

By mid-afternoon, Medina's Charley Company and Bravo Company had met on their sweeps from east to west and west to east, leaving behind them a path of death and destruction. They had destroyed everything in their passage. Meeting, they moved northeast toward the beach and near it set up camp for the night.

As the bivouac was being staked out, a radio message came in from LZ Dottie for Medina. He was told that there had been reports of massive civilian casualties at what the army called My Lai (4). Colonel Henderson, the new brigade commander, had been over the area for some time in a helicopter, checking out his new command and its performance. He had seen, he says, six or seven bodies himself while hovering over Son My village, but "I knew that sometimes civilians get killed accidently in a war."

Such reports, however, disturbed some of the higher officers at LZ Dottie, and Medina was ordered to take his company back to Xom Lang and check the reports and then call in with his findings. But before he could do anything to implement the order, a voice broke in over the radio. It was that of Major General Samuel Koster, commander of the American Division (and now commandant at the United States Military Academy at West Point). Koster was in a helicopter hovering over the area on an inspection tour. He, too, had wanted to check out the performance of this element of his command. To him the ground did not look appetizing and he told Medina not to take his company back "into all that mess" at this late hour of the day.

Koster's countermanding the order did not displease Medina. He was not looking forward to a trip back toward the hamlet, possibly through mine fields and through an area where snipers might be hidden. And he was certainly not looking forward to making the trip back to examine what would be found at Xom Lang.

So the bivouac was established and in the heat of the late afternoon, a number of the men from Charley Company and Bravo Company stripped and went swimming in the waters of the South China Sea, on beaches where in the past sun and pleasure seeking Vietnamese had played. In the waters they washed the smoke and the dirt and the blood from their bodies.

And late in the afternoon, as the Americans vanished at last from Xom Lang, the survivors, those who had hidden through the day, began to creep from their shelters in bunkers overlooked and from the nearby fields and consider the desolation around them.

For most of the day, Pham Phon, his wife and three children had been hiding beneath the bodies of their dead neighbors in the canal. In a low voice he had constantly warned his children to make no noise. But his seven year old daughter, a bullet through her arm and the blood welling up through and around the wound, had occasionally broken the silence with sobs and meek cries of pain and fright. All around them there were other cries of pain and anguish as well from the dying, so that her muffled sounds, the sounds of a small child, were smothered among the louder ones. And the import of the warning came to all of them sometime after shooting had stopped when American voices were heard at the edge of the canal and then several more shots were fired into the bodies and then many of the cries stopped and there was the silence of death all around.

Finally, in the afternoon when he thought it safe, Phon led his family carefully from the canal, crawling to a bunker outside a nearby burning house. They hid in the bunker until nearly dark, when it seemed that all the Americans were gone. Inside the bunker, they bandaged the little girl's arm with torn strips of cloth and tried to comfort her.

At last they left the bunker and began hurrying toward the road and west to safety. As they started down the road, Phon could see in the distance where his house had once been. Now there were only ashes.

Have you ever been back to Xom Lang?

"The next afternoon. About four o'clock I returned. Everything was burned. Then I leave for good and I have not been back again."

How do you feel about what happened?

"Those who are the survivors, they must take care of their own kids and their own lives, and they must not bother. They must not have any ideas about GI's. And I, myself, I am too illiterate to know why it happened."

Nguyen To had hidden in the rice paddies all day, digging himself deeper and deeper into the wet earth as the shots resounded in the air, as the smell of burning filled every pore. Finally there was silence. He rose and looked out to where Xom Lang had been. Now there was only smoke and ashes and the glowing embers of fire, and the smell of smoke and burning flesh. And all around there were the dead, animals and people, his neighbors. When he reached what had been his home, he found only a pile of dust and ashes and ruins. There was nothing living about. He began to stumble through Xom Lang, calling for his wife and sons. In the middle of the hamlet he saw a pile of bodies. Fearfully he approached them. Among the bodies were those of his wife and his ten year old youngest boy.

Later he found his older sons and together they made their way west to Quang Ngai. A few days later the ARVN came and arrested him and put him in prison as a VC sympathizer.

Nguyen Chi came home to the ruins of her house about three in the afternoon. In the yard near the ashes was a body, one of her neighbors. "But I could not find my house," she says. "There was nothing there anymore."

Her family had disappeared as well, and she began searching frantically through the hamlet for her husband and her children. Suddenly, from the fields, she saw her three sons and their cow emerging, moving, running toward her. They had hidden, they told her, all that day and once when they raised their heads an

American soldier had warned them to be quiet and remain hidden.

But still there was no sign of her husband. Some people nearby "told me that a lot of people were killed in the canal." Nguyen Chi hurried to the first canal. "There were lots of people killed there. I saw a wounded baby crying. An old lady, my neighbor, told me, 'You must help the baby. Help to save the baby.' But I was too busy. I must find my husband."

She searched among the bodies in the first canal, but her husband was not among them. Almost in a daze, she wandered away, toward a second canal about a hundred meters beyond. "In the second canal, I find my husband. He was shot. And there were five other people killed in the canal with him, in that part of the canal. There were others dead a little way away in the canal, but I did not stop to count them or to see who they were."

With her children's help, she removed her husband's body from the canal and carried him to the small graveyard at the edge of the hamlet, the graveyard across which Medina had run when he first arrived that morning. There they buried him.

"I never hear of GI's killing people like this before," Nguyen Chi says and shakes her head. "The previous times the GI's were very friendly to the people and the people were very friendly to them. But we are only a miserable people, and perhaps though this is cruel, a cruel action of the GI's, too cruel, perhaps it is war. But now I must raise my children and it is a hard thing. I have no husband any more, and I have no compensation for my husband's death. It is war. It is just war."

About seven that night, Ngo Ngo Thininh returned from her flight west to the ruins of Xom Lang. Near what had been Mr. Sam's house—Mr. Sam who had escaped from the VC prison to return to his home, Mr. Sam who had a son, Ngo Ngo Thininh's husband, in the ARVN, Mr. Sam who was convinced that the

Americans were his friends—she saw her father-in-law and her own father, standing in shock and bewilderment, staring at the ruins. All around them there was death.

In the ashes of the house, she could see the charred remains of some bodies. They were, she was told, the bodies of her younger brothers, shot while they were emerging through the doorway. At that moment, she says, she had a picture in her mind of her little brother as he had been that morning in the kitchen with his bowl of rice and his spoon as the first shells fell. Now he was an unrecognizable charred shape.

Out behind the house, as she wandered dazedly, she saw the carcasses of two water buffalo, slaughtered. Nearby was the body of her mother-in-law, Mr. Sam's wife, shot several times. There were other bodies in the yard and she recognized two of them as her sisters.

All feelings drained from her, she numbly followed Mr. Sam and her father as they wandered through the dead hamlet. They found themselves at the canal. There were other people there, too, moving among the bodies, trying to discover relatives. Ngo Ngo Thininh, Mr. Sam and her father joined them. Among the mass of dead she found her sister-in-law and her two nephews, one twelve and one four. Still alive in the canal near them was her brother-in-law. But he had been seriously wounded, and would die a few days later in the hospital at Quang Ngai. And a short distance away was the body of her mother.

Ngo Ngo Thininh, married to an ARVN soldier, found six members fo her own family slain that day and five members of her husband's family.

The bodies were taken from the canal and from the yard of the house. She helped her father bury the six dead from her family in a single grave. Nearby, Mr. Sam labored and dug separate graves for his own dead.

And then they left Xom Lang for the last time and went to seek shelter among the refugees in Quang Ngai.

About seven that evening, Do Thing An also returned to the hamlet after a full day away. She was completely unprepared for what she found, for she had departed before the shelling started. At sixteen, she had been given the job of shopping for the family that Saturday and she had left almost at dawn for the market at Chau Thanh. When she came home, there was nothing left.

"My house was burned," she says, "and the people told me that my parents had been taken to the canal. I went there. Both my parents had been killed, one of my sisters and her three children had been killed. They were lying with all the other dead people in the canal."

That evening, the relatives of the dead gathered their bodies and buried them, some near where they had fallen, others in the cemetery. The next day, people came from hamlets in the next village to the west, Son Thanh, to help bury in mass graves the bodies of those who had no living relatives left to mourn them, the bodies of whole families wiped out.

And then the people, singly and in small groups, abandoned Xom Lang and all of Son My.

One comes away from these people with the Lamentations of Jeremiah ringing in the mind: "Is it nothing to you, all ye that pass by? Behold and see if there be any sorrow like unto my sorrow, which is done unto me, wherewith the Lord hath afflicted me in the day of his fierce anger."

"They keep saying 'innocent civilians' were involved," says Private Leon Stevenson. "But over there you have to be on one side or the other. How do you draw the line between killing innocent civilians and killing as a part of war?"

As darkness fell that night over Xom Lang, over Son My, over all of Vietnam, it was morning half a world away, in Washington, D.C. If the repercussions of what had happened that morning in this one corner of Vietnam had not yet reached the American capital, repercussions of Vietnam itself, of all that had led up to that morning in the war, had reached the center of government of the United States.

Senator Eugene McCarthy and his young idealists, the advocates of the "New Politics," were celebrating the victory earlier in the week over Lyndon Johnson in the New Hampshire Democratic primary. Eugene McCarthy, until then not a well-known national politician, had upset the incumbent President, the leader of his own party. The issue which he had raised to win that victory was that of the war in Vietnam.

In the caucus room of the United States Senate, Robert Francis Kennedy was about to declare that he was a candidate for his party's presidential nomination, that he, too, would take on the President, his brother's Vice President. And the quarrel which had led to this break was the war in Vietnam, what the United States under Lyndon Johnson had done to Vietnam and what it had done to itself.

In the White House, the President was in an anguished personal struggle. As a result of the war in Vietnam, the people had turned against him, had lost confidence in his ability to lead the nation. Less than four years after he had won the greatest political victory in American history as a candidate of peace, even the voters of his own party had rejected him, now identified as the candidate of war. Within two weeks, he would make his fateful decision. He would stop the bombing of North Vietnam. He would seek a beginning of peace negotiations. And he would not seek re-nomination or re-election as President of the United States. He, too, had been destroyed by the war in Vietnam.

But on that March 16, 1968, Xom Lang and Binh Dong and My Hoi, My Lai and Son My and Pinkville were names that these political leaders had never heard. They were names that most of the military in Vietnam had never heard.

There had been a minor engagement there that day. On the next day and in the days to follow, it would be hailed as a victory.

But the target of the day, the Viet Cong soldiers, had been untouched. From their camp at My Khe sub-hamlet they had heard, early in the morning, the sound of planes and guns to the west; they had heard the sounds moving across the village as the day progressed. And before the Americans came near to My Khe—My Lai (1) or Pinkville—the VC had faded from the scene, moving silently out of the hamlet and north to the sanctuary of Batangan. They would be back.

PART FOUR

The Ultimate Responsibility

THE following morning brought no further orders from LZ Dottie or from Chu Lai to go back to Xom Lang—to My Lai (4). Medina's Charley Company and Bravo Company broke their night camp and continued their sweep through the now almost totally deserted village of Son My.

Before the morning sweep began, Medina sent Calley and the first platoon on a short patrol into the wilderness to the south. The patrol was short-lived. Only a little distance from the bivouac area it stumbled into some mines. One member of the platoon, slightly behind the point, remembers that "all of a sudden there was this explosion and Meadlo went right up into the air."

Meadlo's foot was blown off and he was down, screaming in agony for help. A radio message went back to Medina, from Medina to base and a medevac chopper was on the scene within a couple of minutes to evacuate Meadlo back to the hospital. His war was over. "I felt," he was to say later, "that I was being punished for what I'd done."

Calley, too, was wounded in the mine explosion that crippled Meadlo. But his wound was a minor one and treatment back at the bivouac was all it required to put him back in shape to continue the day's march.

When the first platoon came back to the main body of troops, Medina moved the whole company out, heading south. The men burned and destroyed three more sub-hamlets near the beach, all deserted by their residents, most of them gone within the previous twenty-four hours. At a fourth sub-hamlet on this sweep, the men were in the process of burning the hootches when four Vietnamese were discovered hiding in a bunker. There were two young boys, both teenagers, a woman in her twenties and an older man. John Kinch says that all "were beaten kind of hard" until the youngest pointed to the older man and said he was a VC leader.

According to Medina, the man "didn't look like a rice farmer. He looked like a man who, dressed in a business suit, would look at home in the office." The company's Vietnamese interpreter, Medina says, told him that if he could scare the man enough he might be able to get him to talk. And if, indeed, he turned out to be a VC leader, his information would be extremely useful.

Medina says he emptied his thirty-eight calibre revolver of its bullets and pretended to play Russian roulette against the captive's head. But like all of Medina's actions during this mission, what he says he was doing and what some of his men standing near him say they were sure he was doing run counter to each other. For some members of the company standing nearby are sure that Medina's revolver still had at least one bullet in it and he was playing real Russian roulette with the prisoner. Whether he had bullets in the gun or whether it was empty, the maneuver failed to convince the Vietnamese that he should talk. "He called my bluff," Medina says. "He didn't talk."

So Medina tried another ploy. He tied the man against a palm tree, took his M-16 rifle and began aiming and shooting at the prisoner from fairly close range, trying to hit the tree just along side the man's head. Medina was considered a good shot and this time he proved how good he was. One round slammed into the tree about four inches from the prisoner's head. Another round hit just over the top of the head.

Medina says he then turned to his interpreter and told him to tell the Vietnamese that there would be no more misses; the next shot would be right into the head. Many of the soldiers standing there and watching are convinced that this time Medina was not joking; that he intended to do exactly that. But Medina claims, "If he hadn't talked, I never could have shot him. It is not the normal way of treating prisoners, but I felt that he could give us valuable information."

With his rifle on safety, Medina says, he aimed it at the prisoner's head and began to slowly squeeze the trigger. At that moment, the man began to babble. It turned out that he was indeed a prize—the province chief in Quang Ngai for the National Liberation Front. What he had to say was relayed to an intelligence officer, Capt. Eugene M. Kotouc, who was on the scene.

Then Medina posed for a picture. In one hand he held a coconut, drinking from it. In the other, he held a large knife against the throat of the captive bound to the tree.

There was one more night in Son My. A second peaceful camp near the beach. And then the next morning, the company marched back toward its landing zone; there the helicopters would pick the men up and ferry them back to LZ Dottie.

As they were on the march, Medina received another radio message from the base. Colonel Henderson was coming in with the choppers to talk with Medina. He had heard from a helicopter pilot that there had been needless killing of civilians on the morning of the sixteenth and that Medina himself had shot a civilian woman. He wanted to hear what Medina had to say.

At the landing zone, Medina and Henderson talked as the troops climbed aboard the choppers. "He asked," Medina says, "if there had been any war crimes at My Lai and I told him no." Henderson then asked for Medina's version of the killing of the woman, and the captain told him his story.

"As a soldier," Henderson now says, "I can accept this. It was purely a result of the survival problem you're faced with. You only have a split second to react."

After hearing Medina's story, Henderson got back into his command helicopter and flew back to LZ Dottie while Medina stayed at the field landing zone until all his men were aboard choppers and on their way back to the fire base. Then he climbed aboard the last helicopter for the trip himself, to the end making certain of the welfare of his men.

But whether or not Medina's story had fully satisfied Henderson is doubtful. At any rate, the colonel was still curious as to what had happened on the sixteenth in the sub-hamlet assaulted by his new command. As the men debarked at the fire base, he questioned a number of them, briefly and in a perfunctory manner. They all, he says—and the men agree—assured him that there had been no slaughter of civilians at My Lai (4), that those civilians who had been killed had died mainly as a result of the artillery and chopper barrages, that the "grunts" had done "no shooting up of civilians."

By the time Medina arrived back at LZ Dottie, it was common knowledge that Henderson was around asking questions. Colonel Barker took Medina aside to tell him so. Medina says that he immediately went to his sergeants and asked them whether there had been a massacre. They told him no, and he carried the answer back to Barker, telling him there was nothing to the rumors. Medina says that Barker turned to him and said, "Ernie, you're doing a good job. Go back and run your company."

"As far as I was concerned," Medina adds, "the matter was over."

And indeed it seemed that way. Colonel Barker did no more, and three months later he was killed in a helicopter crash in Vietnam.

About April 1, two weeks after the massacre, Colonel Henderson reported orally to General Koster at Americal headquarters in Chu Lai. The general, too, had heard some rumors about the events of March 16 and he had asked for a report. The colonel told him that his own investigation revealed that nothing untoward had happened in Son My village.

But in Task Force Barker at LZ Dottie, there was some trepidation, some concern that a thorough investigation might somehow be undertaken, and attempts were made by officers to stop the enlisted men from making any moves to precipitate one. It was not, of course, necessary to suggest to most of the soldiers that they remain silent. They knew that if they talked, they would only implicate themselves. In the weeks following the massacre, according to one member of the company, "most of the guys thought it was a great victory."

There were, however, some who had not actively participated and so had nothing to fear if they attempted to expose just what had gone on at Xom Lang, at Binh Dong and at My Hoi. Thus it was deemed prudent to say a few words to them. The most prominent abstainer from the fusillade at Xom Lang had been Michael Bernhardt. He notes that in the days following the Son My slaughter, no one in Charley Company "would talk about it in my presence. I was partially ostracized."

Nevertheless, Medina began to hear stories that Bernhardt was thinking about making the events public. He decided to take the soldier aside and talk with him. One morning, Medina approached Bernhardt at LZ Dottie and told him that he had heard that Bernhardt was planning to write to his Congressman about what had gone on at the hamlet. Bernhardt replied that he had told nobody any such thing, and he had no idea where Medina could have heard the story.

But Medina decided to add a few words anyway. According to Medina himself, he told Bernhardt, "You can write your Congressman if you want to. But you will create a big stink. The matter is being investigated."

If the Army had no desire to pursue the matter any further, there were some others who thought it should be given some publicity. In mid-April, the Viet Cong began flooding Quang Ngai with leaflets asserting that American soldiers had killed many hundreds of civilians in Son My village, though it credited the killings not to Task Force Barker but a unit of the airborne infantry.

Some of these leaflets found their way to Henderson, and he forwarded them to Chu Lai. The result was another request to Henderson for a report to headquarters on the incident, only this time the report should be in writing, not oral. Henderson complied. He wrote that the VC leaflets were nothing but pure propaganda without any basis in fact.

"I didn't attempt to ferret out my information by giving everyone a lie detector test," he says, "nor did I warn a single one of them of their rights. This was not an investigation. It was merely a commander looking over the operations and trying to determine if there was any basis for an investigation." Henderson was sure there was no basis. That was in April of 1968; today he is no longer so sure.

For more than a year, that was the extent of the Army's attempts to find out what if anything had happened in the village of Son My on March 16, 1968.

But the matter was not over for the men of Charley Company. They had to live with what they had done. As the first euphoria of victory passed, some began to become more and more agitated over what they and their friends had accomplished. Some of them got together and discussed briefly writing letters to congressmen or generals or newspapers, somebody, about what had happened. "We just had this feeling," one of them says, "that we couldn't just let it drop there. After we began to think about it a little, some of us began to think maybe we had to do something if we were going to be able to live with ourselves again, to be able to go back into the world."

But since all of them were implicated and might face charges if any investigation resulted from such letters, they eventually, and not without some reluctance, decided to drop the matter right there.

Even if the matter was dropped externally, it could not be dropped internally. Some, of course, were totally unaffected by what they had done and went on much as they had before; they had become so brutalized by the war that brutality was no longer repellent. It was only when they returned to the world at the end of the year, began to see civilized people again and to act as civilians that the import of their acts began to leave its scar.

For others, however, visions of some horror began to haunt their nights. And at least one man found his nightmares so disturbing that he escaped into marijuana and, by August, was spending much of his time benumbed in an opium trance.

For most, though, the war went on, the patrols continued to go out, the hamlets were burned, the people moved, and endless grinding frustration and brutality continued as they had before Son My. After 78 days, Task Force Barker was disbanded; the men left the fire base and went to Chu Lai. Some went to other companies, some stayed in Charley Company and marked the days toward the end of the year when they could return home.

What many did not know then was that a small step had been taken that would suddenly bring the horror of that morning back.

At the end of April of 1968, Ronald Ridenhour arrived at Chu Lai. Walking on the base, he ran into an old buddy he had trained with in Hawaii. The buddy's name was Charles Gruver and he had been in Xom Lang.

Then just over twenty, Ridenhour had grown up in a middle-class home in a Phoenix suburb, gone to Phoenix Junior College and, in 1967, had been drafted when his college work fell below minimum standards. When he arrived in Vietnam as a waist gunner on a helicopter, Ridenhour says, he had little feeling about the war, was certainly not really opposed to it. He was in Chu Lai waiting out a transfer to another unit that day in April when he met Gruver.

"I ran into an old acquaintance of mine at the base camp," Ridenhour says. "Just in the course of conversation . . . you know, telling war stories, 'What have you been doing?' that sort of thing—he said, 'Hey, did you hear what we did at Pinkville?'

"And I said, 'No, what did you do at Pinkville?'

"And it just came out."

Ridenhour didn't quite believe what he was hearing. "Anyone hearing the story for the first time wouldn't quite believe it." But he didn't quite disbelieve it, either. "I left," he says, "thinking, 'God, what if it is true?'"

He decided to see if he could find out if his friend's story really was the truth. In his new unit there were several men who had been in Charley Company at the time of the massacre. Ridenhour sought them out and began to ask questions about March 16. His probing pierced the reticence—or maybe there was a craving to tell someone. He talked with four or five members of Calley's first platoon, he says, at his new station. The stories he got, from each man's own individual view of the morning, checked and corroborated Gruver's story and each other. Ridenhour was convinced that indeed a massacre had taken place.

But the question facing him then was what could he do about it. There was, he says, "a pretty popular story around that it had been investigated and whitewashed." Further, he was sure that anything he did would be automatically discounted; he was not a witness, so whatever he said would be second-hand, hearsay.

So for the moment, Ridenhour did nothing save to continue to confirm in his own mind the fact of the massacre and to amass more first-hand stories from those who were participants. He looked around wherever he was for other men from Charley Company, talked cautiously to them until they began to open up and spin their tales to him. In all, he says, he talked to more than a dozen members of the company. From all he got confirmation, a recital of similar details.

But still he did not know what to do. Finally, in late November, about ten days before he was to be shipped back to the states and discharged from the Army after his year in Vietnam, the catalytic event occurred. In the base hospital at Chu Lai, Ridenhour saw Michael Bernhardt; he had known Bernhardt during training in Hawaii a year earlier, just before both of them had been sent out to Vietnam. Bernhardt was in the hospital recovering from a case of jungle rot on his feet.

After several tentative beginnings, Ridenhour began to tell Bernhardt what he had learned about the massacre at My Lai (4). As he talked, he discovered that his own revulsion, his own feelings that the matter should not be allowed to die, that something should be done to bring the events into the open, were shared by Bernhardt. However, Bernhardt himself was not prepared to push ahead and open what seemed like sealed graves. Ridenhour asked if Bernhardt would back him up if he did something to get an investigation started. Bernhardt answered, yes.

There was still that problem of interesting somebody at a high level who would bring enough pressure to precipitate a thorough investigation, not a cursory one that would result in another whitewash. For the rest of his tour in Vietnam, Ridenhour pondered the question, but those days were too filled with preparations for the return home for him to come to any plan of action. He continued to ponder what he should do during his first months back in Phoenix, a civilian again. He talked with friends at home telling them the story and asking for their advice. Almost all told him the best thing he could do would be to forget it, to keep quiet and not rock any boats.

But Ridenhour was unable to forget it; he had become almost obsessed by thoughts of the massacre being ignored and forgotten. One friend finally suggested that perhaps he ought to follow the story up by writing a letter to the Army's Criminal Investigation Division and asking it to look into what he had heard. Ridenhour thought about this and then dismissed it. He felt that this would merely be asking the Army to investigate itself. And from his own experiences with the Army and nearly a year after the massacre, he felt such an investigation would probably come to nothing.

Still, he could not let go. If no one else were going to do anything about the massacre, he would. If nothing were done, if a massacre, what seemed to him a deliberate and indiscriminate slaughter of innocent Vietnamese civilians, could be dismissed so casually, could be totally ignored to the point of pretending that it had never happened, then something was terribly wrong with his country. If it could be so totally dismissed as though it were nothing, then the whole American adventure in Vietnam would have to be considered some kind of horrible aberration, that what he had learned and always thought about his country might be wrong. If the Army and everyone were going to consider the murder of several hundred Vietnamese civilians— for whose protection the war was theoretically being fought— something that merited not a single word of condemnation or explanation, was something that could even be considered by some a victory, then more than thirty thousand guys—today, more than forty thousand—would have been killed and a couple of hundred thousand more maimed in a war that was worse than meaningless, that was a total perversion of anything and everything for which he and many other Americans thought the country stood.

Ridenhour was convinced that he had to stir the cold ashes of Son My, and the only way to do it would be to enlist powerful support. He sat down and wrote a letter of about fifteen hundred words, detailing everything he had heard about Son My and listing in it the names of those who had told him specific events and those whom they had mentioned. He made thirty copies of the letter and then sent them off to the Army and the Executive and Congressional branches of the Federal Government; to people in government he thought, because of the public stands they had taken on Vietnam, might force action from the Army. The letters went, among others, to the two Senators and three Congressmen from his own home state of Arizona, to Secretary of Defense Melvin R. Laird, to Secretary of the Army Stanley R. Resor, to high officers in the Army itself, and to such Senators as George McGovern of South Dakota, Edward Kennedy of Massachusetts, Eugene McCarthy of Minnesota, J. William Fulbright of Arkansas, W. Stuart Symington of Missouri and Edmund Muskie of Maine.

All the letters were mailed from Phoenix on March 29, 1969 —exactly a year and thirteen days after the massacre at Xom Lang. On April 1, Ridenhour received a long distance telephone call from Democratic Congressman Morris Udall of Arizona. Udall told him that he had received the letter and would do everything in his power to see that some action was taken, and taken promptly, to look into the charges he was making. A couple of days later, Ridenhour received acknowledgments from the other Arizona congressmen and senators that they had received the letter. He received a similar acknowledgment from the Department of the Army. All the others to whom he had sent the letter never replied—though some forwarded their copies to the Defense Department with requests for information.

The letter and Udall's personal intervention undoubtedly stirred the Army from its year-long sleep. On April 18, Ridenhour received another letter from the Army. Now he was told that a full, new investigation into the massacre was beginning. Eleven days later, a full colonel and a court reporter arrived in Phoenix and spent several hours with Ridenhour taking a formal statement from him, essentially repeating what he had said in the letter and adding such other details as he could remember. As the colonel was leaving, he told Ridenhour that the investigation would probably take about two weeks, with another month to six weeks to analyze what was discovered. When they were finished, they would let Ridenhour know the results.

But it was not for more than three months that this initial phase of the investigation came to a close. Secretary of the Army Resor was later to describe what happened to the Senate Armed Services Committee:

"We received identical letters, dated 29 March 1969 and originally addressed to Secretary Laird and five members of Congress, from a Mr. Ronald Ridenhour.

"In these letters, Mr. Ridenhour, a former soldier who had heard rumors of a supposed atrocity from fellow soldiers, alleged that Task Force Barker had been assigned the mission of destroying My Lai and all its inhabitants. He went on to describe in considerable detail, several instances of alleged murder which he believed had occurred there.

"Upon receipt of these letters, the Army immediately initiated a preliminary inquiry, and on April 23, 1969, the Chief of Staff directed the Inspector General to conduct a full-scale investigation of the allegations made by Mr. Ridenhour.

"The investigation took place both here in the United States and in Vietnam and involved interviews with thirty-six witnesses, ranging from the commander of the Eleventh Infantry Brigade to riflemen who participated in the operation.

"On August 4, 1969, the investigation was transferred to the Provost Marshal General. Since that date, criminal investigators have located and interrogated over seventy-five witnesses, twenty-eight of whom are still on active duty. They have also visited the site of the incident and interviewed local Vietnamese officials and former inhabitants of the hamlet who witnessed the alleged killings."

In September, only days before his scheduled discharge from the Army, William Calley was held over for further investigation. He was charged with 109 murders of Vietnamese civilians (the charge was later reduced to murder of 102 civilians).

A few days later Sgt. David Mitchell was charged with intent to kill more than 30 civilians. In January of 1970, Pvt. Gerald Smith, still in the Army, was charged with murder and rape. At the same time, Sgt. Charles E. Hutto, also still in the Army, was charged with murder and rape.

Then, on February 12, 1970, the Army brought twenty murder charges against Lt. (now Capt.) Thomas Willingham, leader of the platoon of Bravo Co. which attacked My Hoi. This was a last minute thing. He was about to receive his discharge when the papers were served. He was the first man to be charged not just with murder but with violation "of the Laws and Customs of War." Such charges stem from international treaties and are the legal basis on which the Nuremberg trials were conducted.

A month later, more charges were brought. Capt. Medina was charged with 4 murders, maiming and assault; Sgt. Kenneth Hodges with rape and assault with intent to commit murder; Sgt. Esequiel Torres with 2 murders and assault with intent to commit murder; Pvt. Max Hutson with murder, intent to commit murder and rape; the intelligence officer assigned to Medina's command, Capt. Eugene Kotouc, with assault, maiming and murder.

And more than thirty-five other soldiers, members of both Charley and Bravo companies, are still under the shadow, the subject of continuing investigations into just what happened that day, and potentially liable to be charged with murder, rape, assault and violation of the "Laws and Customs of War."

After nearly two years, the Army had begun to move, to disinter the grave and look into the unsealed coffin of the dead hamlet.

Though the Army had begun to move, its first brief public announcement on September 6, 1969, that Calley had been charged with the murder of "an unspecified number" of Vietnamese civilians, passed almost unnoticed. Neither the Associated Press, which filed the original story to its press clients, nor the newspapers and broadcasting stations bothered to follow up what should have seemed an intriguing and enigmatic story. *Associated Press* General Manager Wess Gallagher said that the *A.P.* received not "a single call from an individual paper or from broadcasters" asking for more information. But he admits that even without this prodding, his news service should have gone after the story on its own.

One reporter did. Seymour Hersh, a Washington-based journalist, got a call one afternoon from a friend in the Pentagon telling him that there was "a fantastic story" developing at Fort Benning, Georgia, where an army lieutenant was being held for multiple murders of civilians in Vietnam.

Hersh went down to Benning and after several tries managed to talk to Calley. On November 10, he wrote a story about what seemed to have happened at what was then called My Lai. But those to whom he offered the story—Life, Look and other magazines—displayed a total lack of interest. They thought, perhaps, that there was no news in stories of the slaughter of civilians by American soldiers in Vietnam, that this was not something extraordinary to which attention should be called.

Hersh next turned to a friend, David Obst, who had started a small news agency called Dispatch News Service. Obst began making personal telephone calls to newspaper editors around the country. He met with some success, and on November 13, about thirty-five American newspapers printed the first story of the retention of Calley in the Army as a result of charges of the murder of civilians. (On the same day, *The New York Times* ran a similar story of its own which had been tracked down by one of its reporters.)

And so the story of Son My had been disinterred, and opened to the air, it came alive and bore fruit. Meadlo appeared on the Columbia Broadcasting System's television network and told his grisly story under the outraged probing of commentator Mike Wallace. Bernhardt's story, Ridenhour's story and those of other members of Charley Company were detailed by television, radio, newspapers and magazines.

A wave of revulsion seemed to sweep through the nation and around the world. The revelations touched off outraged and self-righteous condemnations, many from countries which had been looking for new and greater causes with which to club the Americans.

The *Times* of London was moved to comment: "Americans, like everyone else, are tempted to hush up scandals. But when they do decide to take the lid off nobody can beat them for thoroughness. This is an occasion when the lid must come off. The charges affect the reputation of the whole American Army. Unless conclusively disproved, they must materially influence the conduct of the war, the negotiations for peace and even the position of President Nixon."

Prime Minister Harold Wilson was under intense pressure in the House of Commons, not only from the opposition but from peace circles within his own Labour Party, to condemn the

American forthrightly and to back off from his unflinching support for American policy.

The Spectator, the conservative London weekly, declared that as a result of the revelations about the massacre, the United States must withdraw completely from Vietnam as "both a necessary act of state and a human imperative."

The French, who had learned with their own blood and their own reigns of terror what colonial wars can do to a nation, showed little compassion for the American dilemma. *L'Express,* the Paris weekly, asserted that, "The Americans have learned that the Americans in Vietnam have become the equal of the French in Indochina, Madagascar, Algeria, and the Germans at Oradour."

An editorial in the socialist daily in The Hague, *Het Vrije Volk,* was blunt in its condemnation: "The Americans have been killing the people they wanted to protect. This means the bankruptcy of United States Vietnam policy."

Throughout the world, the inevitable comparisons were drawn between the American actions in Vietnam and those of the Nazis at Lidice and Babi Yar.

At home in the United States, there was an equal outpouring of both public and editorial comment. Senators and Congressmen demanded a sweeping investigation—though House Armed Services Committee Chairman Mendel Rivers of South Carolina castigated not those who had committed an atrocity but those who had revealed it; he seemed sure that it was all communist propaganda designed to discredit the United States.

Sermons at churches and synagogues became a regular thing for several weeks, and even casual strangers talked about it in shocked tones on the streets and on the trains.

The press was equally outraged. In an editorial, *The New York Times* declared: "Recognizing that war is always brutal and ugly, but also remembering their own shocked disapproval of German and Japanese atrocities in World War II, Americans must face up frankly to what has become a severe test of conscience."

Even President Nixon—who, it turned out, had known about the massacre for several months—took time out at his news conference in early December to express his own personal umbrage. "What appears was certainly a massacre," the President said, "and under no circumstances was it justified. One of the goals we are fighting for in Vietnam is to keep the people from South Vietnam from having imposed upon them a government which has atrocity against civilians as one of its policies, and we cannot ever condone or use atrocities against civilians to accomplish that goal."

In those first days as revelation piled on revelation, Paul Meadlo's mother and father seemed to speak for many Americans. His mother declared, "They took him over to Vietnam and they forced him to do what he never would have done. He was never raised up like that." The Army, she said bitterly, had turned "my son into a murderer."

Meadlo's father, himself a former army private, was even more bitter. If he had been given an order to shoot civilians in cold blood, he said, he would have turned and shot the officer who had given him such an order.

But if the voices expressing horror seemed at first to be the voices of the "silent majority," this soon proved an illusion. Only Meadlo's parents in his own home town in Indiana seemed to be disturbed by what he had revealed. The majority seemed to feel that, "He was under orders. He had to do what his officer told him." And, "The only thing I blame Paul David for was talking about this on television. Things like that happen in war. They always have and they always will. This sort of thing should have been kept classified."

Ridenhour, too, felt the brunt of public anger over his role in baring the deed. At first, mail to him was favorable, but within a couple of weeks, he was getting letters asserting, "I want to tell you, you are a treator [sic], a dirty boy, a Hanoi agent, a Communist, the shame of our society and I wish very soon God kills you." There were others telling him that "only a Jew can be so low and stinking as to side with our enemies and denounce his buddies." Ridenhour, as it happens, is not Jewish.

And there were letters to the newspapers and to the news magazines in a similar vein. One writer to *Newsweek* forthrightly claimed that "any 'innocent civilian' who thinks he can feed, clothe, shelter and otherwise succor the communists in their organized subversion and at the same time expect treatment different from that which he received at Pinkville, ought to have his rice bowl examined."

A poll by *Time* early in January of 1970 revealed that the majority of Americans felt "considerable sympathy" for Calley, and that "surprisingly, Americans are not particularly disturbed by the disclosure that United States troops apparently massacred several hundred South Vietnamese civilians, reasoning that incidents such as this are bound to happen in a war."

But in South Vietnam, itself, the government of President Nguyen Van Thieu denied that any massacre had ever occurred.

Though the South Vietnamese press remained almost totally silent for some weeks after the first disclosures, politicians in Saigon were well aware of what was being revealed about Son My outside their country. Members of the opposition to the government, under the leadership of Senator Tran Van Don, demanded a public investigation and began conducting one on their own. Don toured the area, talked to survivors and came up with enough evidence to convince him and others that something pretty terrible indeed had happened.

One of the worst horrors, Don said, was that "the population floats between the communists and the government, which does not protect them."

As the evidence continued to mount, even Vice President Nguyen Cao Ky thought there might be something to the stories. He intimated that he was enough concerned to think that a deeper look ought to be taken by the government.

But not Thieu. In the imperious manner which has more and more reminded observers of the attitude struck by Ngo Dinh Diem in the years before his downfall, Thieu attempted to end all discussion. He asserted that stories of a massacre were "totally false" and were only Viet Cong propaganda.

He then had the Vietnamese Defense Ministry issue a formal statement: "More than a year ago, on March 16, 1968, the Americal Division launched an operation organized by the Task Force Barker at hamlet My Lai, village of Son My, district of Son Tinh, province of Quang Ngai, aimed at destroying an important communist force there.

"When soldiers of the Task Force Barker engaged into the target, they met strong resistance from the enemy. This hamlet was organized by the communists into a good combat hamlet with good communication and an underground system. The population of the hamlet was forced by the communists to stay in their places.

"The encounter resulted in 125 enemy killed and also there were around 20 civilians killed during the fighting because of the artillery.

"Therefore, reports of newspapers and of the foreign press in the past days which said that there were 567 civilians killed were totally untrue."

The facts, however, disputed the Thieu claims.

Why, then, did Thieu decide to deny the massacre which even the Americans were admitting? There can be no conclusive answer, as there can be no conclusive answer to many other questions about the massacre and about other aspects of the war in Vietnam. But some things are evident.

There is not much popular support in Vietnam for the Thieu regime—and, indeed, its credibility among the populace was further damaged by this very statement which many people knew was false. The government is propped up by the American military establishment both in Vietnam and in Washington, and without this American backing and the American presence in the country, there seems little doubt among most experienced observers that Thieu would fall within days.

If American public opinion, disgusted by the revelations of what had happened at Son My—and what was happening to American men when they went to war in Vietnam—forced the President to accelerate the withdrawal of American troops from Vietnam, the Thieu government would be in grave danger of collapse. Therefore, it seems more than likely, Thieu reasoned that by denying that Americans had murdered his people, he could win further and even stronger support from the American military. And if he could persuade enough Americans that nothing had happened, that American soldiers rather than killing Vietnamese civilians were killing Viet Cong and were protecting and saving democracy in Vietnam, then perhaps there would be no danger of American troops leaving his country—a departure which would necessarily mean his departure as well. The longer he could hold American military support in large numbers within Vietnam, the longer he could remain in power.

Depending not on the support of his own people for the maintenance of power but rather on the support of the Americans, Thieu was willing, even anxious, to protect the Americans and their reputations—even if, at the same time, he alienated his own people and proved to many of them that he would take no steps to protect them from American excesses, that his government was indeed what the Viet Cong was declaring it to be—

nguy chinh phu, a puppet of the United States. But this did not seem to bother Thieu, for he did not—and does not—need the support of the people to continue in power and the people cannot force him from power; all he needs is the continued backing of American military might.

But neither Vietnamese nor Americans gave much credence to Thieu's denial of a massacre and his staunch defense of American soldiers. Even those Americans at home who were most sympathetic to Calley, to Medina and to Charley Company as a whole, who thought that this might have been an accident of war or that there was nothing wrong with what had happened, even they believed despite Thieu that something had happened.

It was beyond dispute that an enormity had indeed occurred at Son My village on March 16, 1968. And even the United States Army at long last, though not without considerable reluctance, seemed to be trying to find out just what had happened and to punish at least those directly involved.

The Army appointed Lt. Gen. William R. Peers, chief of reserve components, to conduct an investigation of the events of that day and whether there had been a deliberate cover up by the original investigation. Peers was given a small staff and several civilian lawyers. The Peers panel heard 398 witnesses, including Calley, Medina, Mitchell, Ridenhour, Bernhardt, and the members of Bravo Company before it ended its investigation. It spent about ten days talking with Vietnamese, both officials and survivors, and visiting the scene of the massacre with an armed patrol. But everything the Peers group did was done behind closed doors, secretly, and it does not intend to release any finding at least until after the trials of those charged. Some who appeared before the Peers group say that the attitude of the panel, and especially Gen. Peers, was suspicious and belligerent toward anyone relating stories of the massacre, with a constant stream of sharp questions—almost like the disbelieving cross-examination of prosecutors—fired in a pre-emptory manner to befuddle and confuse; the committee demanded exact quotations of what Medina and Calley had said, exact locations of where things had happened and expressed annoyance or disbelief at general statements, comments about the mass hysteria of the hour leading to general confusion and uncertainty about reading maps.

While the eventual outcome may prove them wrong, some of the soldiers who testified before the Peers committee came away convinced that its object was to whitewash as best it could, to narrow the responsibility to the lowest possible level, and to discredit the motives of those who had revealed information.

While the Peers group was moving on one level, the Army began to move against Calley, Medina, and other members of Charley and then Bravo Companies on the basis of the separate investigation conducted by the C.I.D. Such steps, however, have raised a variety of very tricky legal questions, and Calley's lawyer, George W. Latimer, one of the best military legal experts in the business, a former judge on the Court of Military Appeals and one of the counsels to the Green Berets in that murder case which was eventually dropped, has not been slow in finding and raising them.

There is, first, the question of Calley's retention in the Army beyond the date scheduled for his discharge—and the retention of other soldiers. Latimer maintains that such a retention is unconstitutional. Calley, he says, should have been discharged when his enlistment expired, and so the court-martial has no jurisdiction over him. In the past, the United States Supreme Court has ruled that courts-martial have no jurisdiction over discharged service men.

Latimer has also struck out against the publicity surrounding the charges against Calley—and the lawyers for others charged have done the same. Because of the widespread discussions of the massacre, Latimer maintains—and with some weight—it may be impossible for Calley or other defendants to receive a fair trial by an impartial jury. He has asked, therefore, for the dismissal of all charges against Calley.

In mid-February, Lieutenant Colonel Reid W. Kennedy, the military judge at Fort Benning, ruled against the Latimer arguments. He held that the Army still retained jurisdiction over Calley and he tentatively set a date in mid-May for the beginning of a court-martial of the lieutenant on the murder charges.

Using this ruling as a basis, the Army will press ahead against the other accused soldiers still in the service.

The question, however, is what can be done with those soldiers who have already been discharged. Can anything be done to bring them before the bar of justice?

There are three alternatives open to the government, none of them easy. It could, first, establish a "military commission," that is, a special military tribunal distinct from a court-martial, to try civilians for war crimes. This has been done in the past—during the Mexican War, the Civil War and World War II. And the Supreme Court upheld such military commissions in a 1945 case involving a Japanese commander in the Philippines who had been convicted by such a tribunal for violation of the "law of war." An American civilian in Japan was convicted by such a commission in 1952 in a case involving negligent homicide.

Such commissions generally apply the "common law of war" to those appearing before them. This common law of war is based on largely unwritten principles of international law dealing with what are considered legitimate acts in wartime and what are considered atrocities. Such a commission could be set up by the President or by the Secretary of the Army.

Though the commission may be the most viable means of trying the men now out of the Army and charged in the massacre, it does have some technical failings which may eventually preclude its use. There are legal questions as to whether a commission can be established anywhere outside a combat zone; and there are also major questions as whether such a commission may be impaneled in cases where there has been no declared war, as in Vietnam.

If the commission proves unfeasible, there are two other means of bringing the men of Charley and Bravo Company to trial, though neither would seem as likely of success. The first would be the establishment of special Federal courts to try ex-servicemen for crimes committed while they were in the service yet not discovered until after they had been discharged. This, however, would mean the imposition of *ex post facto* laws and jurisdiction, and so might well prove unconstitutional.

The third method would be the establishment of an international tribunal to try the men under the Nuremberg Laws. The Nuremberg doctrine was promulgated in 1946 after the trials of Nazi war criminals to provide a legal method for bringing future war criminals to justice. But such tribunals have never been established under the Nuremberg doctrine and there is some doubt not only as to whether they could be formed for this case but also whether the United States would relinquish jurisdiction over its former soldiers.

Regardless of the method by which Calley, Medina, and the others are tried, many legal experts wonder whether he and the other soldiers can be convicted. There is the basic question of what evidence, what witnesses the government can bring to testify against them. Any member of the platoon—save Bernhardt and Olson, who refused to participate in the massacre—who testifies against Calley, Medina or anyone else will be testifying as well against himself, and the lawyer will not be slow to point this out. While documentary and circumstantial evidence will be available to the prosecution—that Vietnamese civilians had been killed, that Calley's platoon had been in the hamlet at the time of the killing—direct evidence of who had done what will depend upon one soldier pointing his finger at another—and if that happens, there will certainly be an interchange of, "If I did that, you did this."

Vietnamese witnesses will probably be next to useless in such a trial, for, as Vietnamese often say, they can't tell the difference between one soldier and another.

Where there is communal guilt, where one man's testimony will not only convict another but also himself, the success of any prosecution must be considered highly doubtful. Even after the Army and the Government find the means to bring Medina, Calley, Willingham and Charley and Bravo Companies to trial, and if they are convicted, there will still remain a number of unanswered questions, many of which the Army undoubtedly does not want to face. Some of these questions may strike right to the core of just how such an event could occur. The purpose of justice in this case will not be served by punishing a handful of men if we do not discover at the same time why the massacre took place and whether such a slaughter can be prevented in the future.

There are at least four major questions which emerge from the events of that March 16th:

(1) How could the massacre be kept a secret for so long? Did nobody outside Charley Company and the survivors know about it?

(2) Did the army cover up and whitewash the company in its initial investigation?

(3) Who gave the orders that precipitated the massacre?

(4) Was the massacre at Son My unique, an aberration in the American involvement in Vietnam?

How could the massacre be kept secret for so long? Did nobody outside Charley Company and the survivors know about it?

Far from being a secret, the massacre was well known both to

Americans and to Vietnamese.

As the experiences of Michael Bernhardt and other members of the group demonstrate, the soldiers in Charley Company were not reticent about talking of Son My when they ran into friends, like Ronald Ridenhour, in Vietnam. These friends told other friends. There were rumors all over Chu Lai and elsewhere in Vietnam soon after that March 16th that a massacre of Vietnamese civilians had occurred, with many of the details well substantiated.

Further, when the soldiers from Charley Company returned home, many of them told friends and families what had happened. And again, these friends told other friends.

If the massacre was a secret among Americans, it was a secret shared by a vast number of gossips.

Among Vietnamese, particularly in Quang Ngai Province, there were few who had not heard the story, with many details, of what had happened on that March morning.

Within a month after the massacre, the Viet Cong were flooding Quang Ngai with leaflets giving fairly explicit descriptions of what had taken place—though because the VC cited the wrong American unit as having been the perpetrators, the leaflets may have been discredited by many.

But the VC were not the only source of the reports of what had happened at Xom Lang. There were survivors, both of the sub-hamlets and of the whole village. Many—and none can be sure exactly how many—had been wounded during the shooting and had not died. They, or at least some of them, were treated in hospitals at Quang Ngai and elsewhere in the I Corps area.

Pham Di, who was seriously wounded, was taken to a Quang Ngai hospital by his wife after the Americans left Xom Lang. Still bedridden and feeble in his refugee-camp hootch, Pham Di says, "The doctors and the nurses asked me, 'Why are you wounded?' I told them, 'GI's operate in my hamlet and shot at me and I was wounded.' " A few days later, his wife returned to the hospital to visit him and told the nurses and the doctors that a great many people were killed during an American attack on her hamlet, Tu Cung, and her sub-hamlet, Xom Lang.

"So the nurse came in and treated my wound again," Pham Di says, "and she asked me what happened. I told her that GI's had killed more than three hundred people in my hamlet."

An American doctor later arrived to examine Di's wound and ordered him prepared for an operation. But the American seemed totally uninterested in discovering how Di had been wounded—perhaps because he had already seen in Vietnam so many Vietnamese civilians suffering from severe wounds.

What happened with Di happened again and again with other wounded survivors. Those who were not wounded also divulged the story. Ngo Ngo Thininh and Mr. Sam told the young ARVN soldier who was her husband and his son. He in turn told members of his company of ARVN.

A young bureaucrat at the government office in Quang Ngai said that within days after the massacre a number of people from Xom Lang came in to see him, since he had been born in the sub-hamlet. "They told me that some of my relatives had been killed during the operation by the GI's."

Did they tell you what had happened?

"Yes. They said the bombs and shells had fallen, then the GI's came and shot the people. One of those killed was the head of my family name."

These reports soon reached provincial Vietnamese officials. Captain Tran Ngoc Tan, the district chief at the time of the massacre, heard about it quickly and passed the information on to the province chief after confirming the story in less than a week's cursory investigation. Captain Tan told Colonel Thon That Khien, the province chief, that soldiers of the Americal Division had killed about five hundred civilians in the hamlet. He even compiled a list of possible victims—those known dead and those missing—but the list seems to have disappeared some-where between Tan's office and Khien's.

Nevertheless, Colonel Khien began another investigation of his own. At first, he said, he doubted the truth of the story and thought it was merely enemy propaganda. As he dug deeper, he became convinced that something had indeed happened, on the order that Captain Tan said, and he passed the report on to the commander of the Second ARVN Division in Quang Ngai. What happened after that within the South Vietnamese army and government circles is unknown, but if the report had followed normal channels, it would have reached all the way to President Thieu within a matter of a month or so.

However, when the renewed interest in the massacre was awakened, Colonel Khien met with some reporters in Quang Ngai. He told them that he thought that indeed civilians had been killed, perhaps unnecessarily, during the operation. But remaining utterly circumspect, he expressed some doubt whether the total number of casualties had reached five hun-dred; he was not prepared to say how many had been killed. Nevertheless, Khien's statement went counter to the official Thieu-Vietnamese government line that nothing at all had hap-pened. And so, within a few days, Khien was transferred to a backwater from his post as province chief in Quang Ngai.

The story of the massacre, then, was well known among people in Quang Ngai and probably among many Vietnamese in the government as far away as Saigon.

Even some American civilians in Quang Ngai city knew that something had happened, though they were not sure, they say, exactly what. "It's not surprising that we don't know all that happens around here," says one American province adviser in Quang Ngai, R. F. Hill. "Only the insiders get information from the Americal Division, and we're not those insiders. Since that was VC country, we just didn't go up there. The province chief

knew that something had happened. But it was all very vague."
Of course, many Vietnamese just do not tell Americans what
they know.

A British doctor, Alje Venemma, was working in a private
hospital run by a Canadian medical team in Quang Ngai at the
time of the massacre. Dr. Venemma says that he is "amazed" by
the American statements that they did not know what had
occurred. He says that a high Vietnamese official told him of the
killings one day at the hospital, and he is certain that the Americans were told, too. But, Dr. Venemma adds, he had become so
inured to the deaths of civilians on a large scale that he had not
thought the stories about Son My particularly out of the ordinary.

Thus, there was no secret either among Americans or Vietnamese about the mass murder at Son My.

*If there was no secret, then did the Army attempt to cover up
and whitewash the massacre?*

There seems to be no question that the Army did, indeed,
attempt to whitewash the Company and cover up the massacre
by closing its eyes to it.

With the story running uncurbed among both American
troops who came in contact with Charley Company and among
Vietnamese in Quang Ngai, there can be no other explanation
for the Army's failure to conduct more than a cursory examination of the events. It did not question Vietnamese or more than
just ask a few innocuous questions.

The American authorities merely quizzed Captain Medina and
members of his company, none of whom could be expected to
have incriminated themselves by admitting participation in the
carnage. No one from the Army C.I.D. or the intelligence corps
(who must certainly have heard many stories of what happened
from Vietnamese in the course of gathering intelligence data)
questioned any survivors. No attempt was made by the Army to

send investigators to Xom Lang to examine the scene of the massacre. A few, simple-minded questions were asked of the men who had taken part in the slaughter, men who could under no conceivable conditions be expected to admit what they had done, and then the matter was dismissed with the report that rumors of a massacre were groundless.

Perhaps it would have been asking for more than the Army was willing to give to expect anything else. After all, this was shortly after the end of the Tet Offensive. Morale among American soldiers in Vietnam, never at the highest, was then at a nadir. Many in the army felt—and many still do feel—that to conduct an investigation, a thorough and searching one, into an atrocity, and to bring charges of murder, rape and other horrendous crimes against American soldiers involved, would have served only to lower morale even further. To bring into question what was then and is still basic military doctrine in Vietnam—the search-and-destroy mission and the establishment in the rural countryside of the free-fire zone—would have called into question the entire American actions in Vietnam since the U.S. involvement began.

There is no question but that the Army seemed convinced that the company had attacked and wiped out a center of Viet Cong strength and those killed may well have been, however tenuous the connection, associated with the VC. After all, the Army's policy throughout Vietnam, as demonstrated by leaflets showered over the country and by the messages blared over helicopter loudspeakers, was that those people who gave any aid and comfort to the VC could expect retribution from the Americans; their villages and hamlets destroyed and themselves killed.

Under this directive, civilian casualties during these search-and-destroy missions had become the rule in Vietnam rather than the exception. Though this might be counter to official policy from Washington, every military man, in Vietnam and in the Pentagon, knew that whenever Americans took to the field in search-and-destroy operations, the odds were much better than even that Vietnamese civilians would be killed and wounded. Thus a thorough-going investigation of any one of these operations, one that was considered nothing out of the ordinary, but which may have resulted in somewhat excessive killing, would have brought into sharp focus and question the Army's activities all over the country.

Again, the question of what such disclosures would have meant in the political climate at home was crucial. Any complete investigation and later criminal actions would most certainly have been widely covered by the press and television—as they were when the story finally broke—and would have received considerable publicity back in the United States. At that time, in early and mid-1968, the protests against the war in the United States had reached a peak. Senators Eugene McCarthy and Robert Kennedy, campaigning on peace platforms, had defeated President Johnson in Democratic Party primaries and forced him to relinquish ambitions for a second term. The demonstrations against the war had rallied and split the nation as it had not been divided within memory. The Army had no desire to give further ammunition to the war protestors. Any revelations at that time about the events at Son My would surely have led to renewed and enlarged marches and protests at home and to swelling demands for an end to the war or the total withdrawal of all American troops.

Whether these considerations were consciously thought out by the military in Chu Lai, or elsewhere, there is some evidence that officially the story did not go beyond the Americal Division's headquarters. Yet some military leaders in Saigon certainly must have heard of it; indeed, there was a rumor for a time that a report had reached General Westmoreland and that he did not want it to be spread about, but this is denied. What is certain beyond question, is that the military did not want to find out officially what had happened, that it did not want to learn the details, and that it made no real effort to learn the truth, that it assumed an ostrich-like posture. Nearly two years after the event, Colonel Henderson, who had taken command of the brigade the day before the massacre, could still say, "Up until two weeks ago, I would have sworn it could not happen without my knowing about it." Colonel Henderson officially did not want to know and made no effort to find out, any more than did any other high American military official want to know or make any effort to learn. Whether Colonel Henderson did, in fact, know what had happened is another question.

The original military investigation, then, did exactly what it had set out to do. It was looking for an answer that would say: "There had been no massacre." By restricting its search only to mild questions directed at participants—one member of the company says he was asked, "There wasn't any killing of civilians at My Lai, was there?"—and ignoring those like Bernhardt who had not taken part in the killing—Bernhardt was never questioned in this original investigation—the Army got precisely the answer it wanted.

Who gave the orders that precipitated the massacre?

We can, first, attempt to narrow this question to its most limited nature: were there orders to kill everyone in this hamlet? If so, who gave them?

One way of discovering this is, first, to narrow and restrict the search by process of elimination. The individual soldiers at Xom Lang did not, of course, take it upon themselves to conduct a slaughter. They operated under orders. Almost everyone at the scene says that he was told to destroy everyone and everything in the hamlet.

At the top Colonel Henderson and General Koster can initially be absolved from the immediate charge. The general, operating from American headquarters in Chu Lai, was concerned with a variety of other actions, not just the details of a single minor operation by one of the many task forces under his command. Then, Colonel Henderson had just taken command of Task Force Barker the previous day. While he was consulted about the operation, it had been planned before his arrival and he was more a bystander than an actual participant in this, his unit's first assault under his command. All this, however, puts aside for the moment the question about an officer's responsibility for the actions of his men, even a general far removed and a new officer who has not yet dealt with the men to any extent. It also puts aside the question of knowledge and ability to stop the action on the part of these high officers.

If for the moment we can remove from immediate responsibility both those at the lowest level—the individual soldiers—and those at the highest level—General Koster and Colonel Henderson—we are left with three men on whom to narrow the focus: Lieutenant Colonel Frank Barker, the task force's executive officer, now dead; Captain Ernest Medina, commander of Charley Company; and Lieutenant William Calley, leader of the first platoon; and Lieutenant Thomas Willingham.

Calley was not the most universally liked or respected officer in the American Army in Vietnam. In fact, as we have seen, many of the men under his command were more than a little wary of him and skeptical of his ability. He had given some of them pause on more than one occasion, and before they left Vietnam he would give them reason to wonder about him a number of times again.

If there was—and there was—some suspicion among his men about Calley's balance and his ability to lead and make decisions in crisis, there was little suspicion about his initiative. Almost to a man, those who served under him say that he displayed little initiative, that he rarely took it upon himself to do anything without checking first with higher officers, that is, with his company commander, Medina. The men became convinced that Calley was a conveyor belt down which passed the orders from on high. Charles West says, "The thing about Calley is that Calley could not give the order to kill everyone. But it's a fact that every GI thought everyone had to be killed in the village. Captain Medina told us that everyone had to be killed." Then West adds, "But he didn't give the order either, because I believe that it had to come from higher up."

Did it, indeed, come from Medina or did it come from higher up, or are there yet other explanations?

Medina freely admits that his speech to the men the night before the attack was designed to stir them up, to get them ready for the next morning when, he was convinced on the basis of the reports from intelligence, they would fight a fierce battle with one of the best VC units in Vietnam. He aroused them with the thought that they would be able to take revenge for the killing and maiming of friends by unseen mines and booby traps, that finally they would face a real enemy, a living one, and would be able to fight him.

There are many who say that during his pep talk, Medina gave the order that everything and everyone in the hamlet should be destroyed, that nothing should be left alive or standing. Medina, of course, maintains that he was convinced that all civilians would be out of the hamlet by the time the Americans arrived. This admission on the part of Medina would indicate that those men who remember him ordering total annihilation are undoubtedly correct; Medina's claim that he thought only the enemy would be there would surely verify this.

There seems no doubt that Medina stirred up the men, put them in the mood to kill the next morning. That a measure, and a large measure of responsibility falls on him for the order and its implementation is undeniable.

But was he, then, the man with whom the order originated, on whom the ultimate responsibility falls?

There is Colonel Barker, now dead, killed three months later in the helicopter accident in Vietnam. What Barker said or didn't say can never be known. But it is certain that the plan of action for March 16th was discussed fully between Barker, Medina and the two other company commanders—of Able and Bravo—and that none of the company commanders took it on their own initiative to give orders to their men of major magnitude without clearing those orders first with Barker.

But again, operating strictly within the framework of the military command in Vietnam and the situation on the ground there, can the ultimate responsibility for the massacre be laid to Barker? Even if the massacre was a terrible blunder?

Barker and Medina were operating on the basis of intelligence reports. It was on this basis that they drew their plans for the assault on March 16th. These reports pointed to a heavy concentration of VC, the 48th Local Force Battalion, at what was referred to in conversation, but nowhere written, as Pinkville.

As we now know, the VC were not at the hamlet which Charley Company attacked on March 16th. They were actually at My Khe sub-hamlet in My Lai hamlet less than three kilometers east to the sea. And as an examination of the Army maps makes patently clear, My Khe was Pinkville: it is shaded in pink on these military maps and is labeled My Lai (1). Vietnamese informants, unaware that the American military listed six My Lai's on its maps, several of them not even in My Lai hamlet, had previously informed the American Army that the VC were in My Lai hamlet. If the Army was after the VC, as it says it was, then the attack was supposed to hit Pinkville. Medina, the soldiers and everyone else constantly talks about Pinkville and about the expected VC concentration there. But the attack did not fall there, but on Xom Lang, labeled My Lai (4), to the west.

On the basis of the intelligence reports, Barker and Medina were convinced that they were going to attack the VC and would fight a major battle, as part of the larger over-all attempt to search, clear and destroy the entire village of Son My.

If the attack was deliberately aimed at Xom Lang—My Lai (4)—and not at My Khe—My Lai (1), Pinkville—then it was a deliberate slaughter of civilians, planned to be such from the start and without even the excuse, however tenuous it may be, that the Army expected to fight the VC that morning.

If we assume, however, that the command actually did think it was attacking a VC hamlet, then, in the light of American practice in Vietnam, it was only natural to order the hamlet destroyed. It was a standard order for American troops on search-and-destroy missions to raze the houses and fields, kill the animals and kill any VC discovered, taking only a few prisoners for interrogation. For American troops to go in with guns blazing the next morning, as a result of the intelligence reports that had been passed on to Barker and Medina and the talk given the men by Medina the evening before, was to be expected.

What was not to be expected, and not to be tolerated, was what followed. That was the massacre. Such slaughter could only be carried out if no resistance was encountered. If the VC had been there, waiting, there would have been a major engagement, with heavy casualties taken on both sides. There was no engagement, for there were no VC at Xom Lang; there was no resistance, just the men of Calley's platoon firing and killing everything and everyone.

Here one can, to some measure, point to Calley. He himself has been charged with the murder of more than a hundred of the people in that hamlet; he ordered his men to kill others; and he walked around that hamlet killing and watching the killing.

But on his record as an officer prior to this engagement, it should not have surprised anyone that Calley would obey the orders that had been given him despite the change in circumstances. He was not an officer to deviate, not an officer to initiate or show his own initiative on the ground, and he was undoubtedly as much taken by the spreading mass psychosis of that moment as anyone else in his company. In strict accordance with his orders to destroy the hamlet and all that was in it, he waged war and slaughter with zeal; he carried out his orders with relish and so did many of his men.

If Calley carried out his orders to the letter, displaying a lack of initiative and flexibility that should have been expected of him as an officer—does this, then, absolve either Medina, Barker or, on the higher levels, Henderson and Koster?

It does not. For, again, an officer is supposed to be responsible for the actions of his men. A company is not such a large unit that the commanding officer can realistically be unaware of what its platoons are doing. A company does not operate over such a wide swathe of ground as to be out of contact. And knowing Medina, it is highly unlikely that he would permit one of his platoons to operate on its own, especially in the midst of intense fire, without being in communication and finding out what was going on.

Medina, even if he was on the outskirts of the hamlet throughout the action, was not so far removed as to be unaware, or out of contact with his men. The sound of small arms fire and explosions were intense during the hour when the massacre was taking place. The smoke hung like a pall over the village. There were the shrill screams of the Vietnamese pleading for mercy as they were shot down. These sounds and these sights must certainly have reached Medina; they reached other residents of

Son My a mile or more away, and were so intense that the VC in My Khe—Pinkville—knew something was coming their way and disappeared north into Batangan.

At the same time, Medina was aware that no resistance had been met in Xom Lang. Therefore, he should—and must—have wondered immediately about the intense firing. Unless, that is, he knew exactly what was happening inside the hamlet and had no intention of interfering, of putting a stop to it. He knew Calley and he knew Calley's capabilities. And he had told his men that they would have a chance that morning to take revenge on Vietnamese for their fallen friends.

If Medina, then, was certainly aware of what was going on in Xom Lang, had sparked it himself, and was doing nothing to stop it, there were others as well who must have known that something untoward was happening in the hamlet. Both Barker and Henderson were in helicopters viewing the scene, and so, too, was General Koster. Though initially they might have thought that a major battle was raging below them, such thoughts were shortly dismissed—only one American casualty was reported, that of the man with the wounded foot. And there were bodies all over the ground. Helicopter pilots reported sighting scattered bodies all over the area and inside the hamlet. But it was not until almost everyone in Xom Lang was dead that questions were asked from these command helicopters, questions which ended the slaughter.

There are, then, many answers to the question of who gave the orders for this particular incident and who let it go on to its end, and the reason for those orders. No one in authority, from General Koster to Colonel Henderson to Colonel Barker to Captain Medina to Lieutenant Calley to the lowest private can escape a share of the responsibility for what happened at Xom Lang. And none of them can point to the other and say he was the one most responsible.

But the search for answers cannot stop here. It must go beyond Xom Lang to discover whether this atrocity was unique and why it could happen and whether such a slaughter could recur.

Was the massacre at Son My unique, an aberration in the American involvement in Vietnam?

There is, unfortunately, only one answer that can be given to this question, an answer hard for Americans to accept. The massacre at Son My was not unique, although it may have been the largest such incident of its kind in any one particular location and moment. One is forced to conclude, however reluctantly, that what happened in extremis at Son My is only symbolic of what has happened all over Vietnam since the massive enlargement of the American commitment (from that of non-combat advisers to search-and-destroy warriors): that what happened is endemic to the American military commitment in Vietnam. To say that this is endemic to the American military in Vietnam is not, of course, to excuse or absolve the Viet Cong, the North Vietnamese Army and others for war crimes, for massacres and atrocities of their own. The VC and the NVA, according to enough documentary evidence to establish the validity of the charge, killed between three and five thousand people at Hue during the Tet offensive. The slaughter at Hue, though, was not indiscriminate but, in line with totalitarian practices elsewhere throughout the world, it was aimed at eliminating political opponents and potential opponents.

Until the counting of the dead at Hue—and before the revelations about Son My—the slaughter of Vietnamese civilians at Son Tra, a hamlet north of Quang Ngai city, a hamlet considered pacified at the time, in June of 1968, had been pointed to by the Americans as "the worst Viet Cong atrocity against civilians of the war." The VC had attacked an American Marine CAP team and a Vietnamese Popular Force unit camped next to the hamlet to protect it from such raids. During the fighting, Son Tra took the brunt of VC grenades and small arms fire; the hamlet was eighty-five per cent destroyed, seventy-three civilians and fifteen armed pacification workers were killed and more than a hundred civilians were wounded. But even the American military conceded that in the case of Son Tra, the VC did not deliberately set out to massacre the hamlet; the civilians were caught in the middle of a pitched battle and became unwitting victims of their location.

Aside from Hue, however, massive and indiscriminate slaughter of civilians does not seem to be the kind of war that the VC and the NVA have waged in South Vietnam. In many hamlets, of course, they have assassinated or executed village and hamlet chiefs and other officials. But usually these victims were selected because of their position or person and generally they were not particularly well liked by the people.

While the VC and the NVA have killed thousands of Vietnamese in the more than ten years that this war has been going on, they have rarely been accused of indiscriminate slaughter; rather, the charge most often leveled against them is that they have used murder and terror as weapons to rid themselves of political foes and to frighten the people into supporting them.

And despite what the VC and the NVA, the communists, have done, nothing can absolve Americans, particularly since the Americans have pictured themselves to the world and to themselves as the protectors of the rights and liberties of the people of South Vietnam.

It seems that hardly a week has gone by since the massive American engagement in Vietnam without some charge or another being leveled against Amercians for a massacre somewhere in Vietnam, from the I Corps in the north to the IV Corps in the Delta.

It is only necessary to cite a couple of them. In June of 1968, the Army began an investigation of charges that a company of the Ninth Infantry Division used a civilian village in the Delta for "target practice." The scene was near the division's head-quarters at Dong Tam, southwest of Saigon. At least one Vietnamese civilian was killed during the firing, though there may have been many more. No one seems certain.

In mid-1966, in a well-documented and admitted action, American F-100 fighter-bombers attacked a village in the Delta by mistake and more than twenty-five villagers were killed, another hundred wounded.

In mid-1968, during a fire fight with the VC near Can Tho in the Mekong Delta, American troops again hit the wrong village and killed more than seventy-two civilians, wounding two hundred and forty and destroying four hundred and fifty homes. According to an American officer at the time, "The incident took place at night and our guys did not know who was shooting at them. And they stepped up their firing. Unfortunately, they shot up one of the friendliest and most secure towns, Cai Rang, in the Mekong Delta."

As recently as October of 1969, troops of the Americal Division burned and destroyed thirteen villages in Quang Ngai and Quang Tin provinces in order to "deny the villages to the Viet Cong." How many civilians were killed in the operation no one is prepared to say, but one officer asserted, "If it's all a free-fire zone, you can sit on the hills and see the dinks running around, so they call in a big air strike."

And in what was probably an exaggeration, the Viet Cong delegates to the Paris peace talks charged recently that during "an accelerated pacification program" called Sea Tiger in November of 1969, American, South Vietnamese and South Korean troops had killed more than seven hundred Vietnamese civilians in the villages of Binh Duong, Binh Giang, Binh Trieu, Binh Hoa and Binh Doa in the Thang Dinh district of Quang

Nam Province. Charges of massacres against South Korean troops are almost too numerous to cite; wherever the ROK's have been, such charges have been leveled against them by the civilians; they are, in fact, universally feared by Vietnamese. And the ARVN, too, has been cited for depredations against the civilian population in hamlets on numerous occasions.

But even if all these individual massacres and raids can be discounted—which, of course, they cannot be—still what happened in Son My was not unique and did not occur in isolation. What happened was a direct outgrowth of what the United States has done over the past six years and more in Vietnam, was the inevitable outgrowth of this involvement.

To an essentially localized and limited war fought, despite its ferocity, with certain ground rules—undeclared but nevertheless understood—the United States brought modern military technology and a vast arsenal of sophisticated weapons (excluding nuclear weapons, though one hears from officers the frequent cry that the big mistake of the war was limiting it, not "nuking Hanoi" and Haiphong and the whole countryside). The war was widened to take in the entire country and all the people, and the ground rules for limiting it were thrown into the trash heap.

There has been the indiscriminate use of napalm on hamlets and villages thought to shelter the VC. Napalm destroys villages and kills and maims the innocent along with the guilty, and it is as thorough and nearly as efficient as small arms fire from the ground; but there is little danger of violent response to those using it. Additionally, those who drop napalm, unlike soldiers on the ground, do not have to kill and maim their victims face-to-face; they never even have to see them, unless they happen to wander the streets of a Vietnamese city or go into a refugee camp or children's hospital or orphanage where the faceless, scarred victims of napalm attacks are all-too visible.

There has been the massive bombing by B-52's and other

planes over much of Vietnam. Despite the accuracy of such "strategic bombing," hamlets containing innocent civilians were, and are still being, totally destroyed, and the civilians cower in their homes waiting their destruction, given not enough warning to take to their bunkers and at least obtain some partial protection. There is not a city or a refugee camp in Vietnam without its limbless children and adults, the victims of such attacks. There is not an orphanage in Vietnam that is not filled with the young survivors.

There has been the indiscriminate spraying of defoliants and chemicals throughout the country, to destroy trees and crops and, in the process, to destroy people. The chemicals used on the Vietnamese countryside, supposedly to deny cover and food to the Viet Cong, are chemicals which are barred from use on crops in the United States because of their effects both on crops and on people. They are chemicals which cause gross birth abnormalities, an increasing phenomenon in Vietnam in defoliated areas. Most of the children born of parents subjected to such chemical warfare are hidden, but in Vietnam their existence is no secret.

There have been the declarations of free-fire zones and search-and-destroy missions. These put civilians, who had nowhere to go except to refugee camps to starve and live in misery, at the mercy of American troops. The refugee camps are filled with the victims of such policy, and so are the graveyards.

There has been the total isolation of American troops in Vietnam not only from ARVN soldiers—their theoretical allies who have been totally ignored, deprecated and sometimes even considered part of the enemy—but also from the vast mass of the Vietnamese population. Among Americans there is little if any understanding of the problems facing the Vietnamese. Americans seem to act only under the assumption that any Vietnamese who lives in a free-fire zone, who lives in a contested area, is automatically VC and therefore fair game. No distinction is made by the American military between friend and foe; all Vietnamese are considered foe, and indeed, all of Vietnam seems to be considered part of America, American territory momentarily occupied by hostile elements—the Vietnamese people—who, at any cost, ought to be eliminated.

With such events and such attitudes, a Son My was inevitable.

What had begun, theoretically at least—and what has been so described by all American leaders, from Eisenhower to Kennedy to Johnson and now Nixon—as a war to protect democracy in South Vietnam, to safeguard all of Southeast Asia from the communists; what had been constantly proclaimed as a war to prevent communism from enforcing its will on an unwilling populace; what had begun and has been waged—Americans were told over and over again by Lyndon Johnson, Dean Rusk and William Westmoreland—as a "war for the hearts and minds" of the people of Vietnam, was never that, not once American fire power was brought to bear.

The United States never learned an ancient lesson. As I listened to the South Vietnamese—those who are for the government, those who are neutral and even those who express sympathies for the Viet Cong—I heard a constant refrain. Under the government, they were taxed, lectured and their young men drafted, but mainly they went their own way and were left alone. Under the VC, they were taxed, lectured and their young men drafted, but mainly they went their own way and were left alone. Then the Americans came.

Backed by enormous power, arrogance and a certitude in the righteousness of the cause, Americans came to Vietnam with the pretense of fighting a war for the "hearts and minds" of the Vietnamese. But it was never more than a pretense.

One does not use napalm on villages and hamlets sheltering

civilians caught between the government and the enemy if one is attempting to persuade those people of the rightness of one's cause.

One does not blast hamlets and their occupants to dust with high explosives from jet planes miles in the sky without warning, if one is attempting to woo the people living there to the legitimacy and goodness of one's cause.

One does not defoliate a country and deform its people with chemicals if one is attempting to persuade them of the foe's evil nature and one's own morality.

One does not declare where the people live, in their ancient homes, where all they have is centered, where all they desire is to be left alone by everyone, a free-fire zone with anything and everything in it liable for destruction and death if one is attempting to persuade these people that one is fighting for their lives and liberties.

One does not think of all the people as the enemy, as dinks and gooks and slopes and slants, as sub-human with neither emotions nor desires, with lives controlled at the whim of one's army; and conduct search-and-destroy mission throughout the country with no respect for property or life if one is attempting to convince these people of the rightness of one's cause, of one's respect for their desires and wishes, and attempting to win their allegiance.

The war that the Americans have been fighting in Vietnam— despite all the pretense and all the statements to the contrary— has been a total war. The aim of the war has been victory— though no one has succeeded in answering the question of what will be won by such a victory, what will be left to the victor.

But as historians have pointed out since antiquity, and as American politicians and military leaders have either totally ignored and been ignorant of, the end of war—victory or defeat—is not the end of life. Life continues when the war is who have, if they look, witnessed their country torn by internal dissension over the war as never before—at least not since the Civil War. And they have witnessed, if they looked, their illusions about the rightness and the morality of their nation brought to nothing.

Lyndon Johnson, in the days when he was calling the nation to the struggle, used the analogy of the policeman protecting a man's home from housebreakers. But who has been the housebreaker? And what is the responsibility of the housebreaking policeman now that in his zeal to protect the house he has destroyed it?

And what of Son My today? Horse Mountain has crossed the river and there is no more law and no more peace anywhere in Son My village. There is no more Son My village. Everything was destroyed by the American troops; not a house stands, not a field still flourishes, not an animal grazes. It is uninhabited wasteland.

After the massacre, all the villagers fled. Those who sympathized with the Viet Cong and who were undeterred by the firsthand evidence of what the Americans could and would do in VC-controlled territory, went north to Batangan, deeper into VC country. But most moved south, across the Tra Khuc River, to safer villages, and eventually they joined the march west to join the millions in refugee camps.

Silence spread across what had once been a village. But soon the VC were back. They occupied the abandoned bunkers and dug new ones and, in the night, began raiding from the hamlets again. But now there are no civilians there, only VC. What had cost so dear to clear and pacify remained pacified not at all. Within days of the departure of Task Force Barker, Son My was more hostile than it had ever been, more intensely contested ground where no man was safe. It became the scene for battle after battle. And save near the new refugee camp across the road from where Xom Lang was, it is so even today.

I sit with my friend, the former poet who has become an ARVN major because there is no place for poetry in Vietnam. It is a warm night in Saigon, and so it is pleasant to sit on the terrace of the Continental Palace Hotel and drink a cold drink and watch the motorbikes race down Tu Do, to watch the women in their au dais as they walk gracefully down the sidewalk. It is pleasant to sit and talk here, a little way from the war.

"It would be nice," the major says just before leaving, "if the Americans would go and help defend someone else's freedom for a change."

ST. MARY'S COLLEGE OF MARYLAND

ST. MARY'S CITY, MARYLAND

053714